Handwriting Without Tears
Teacher's Guide

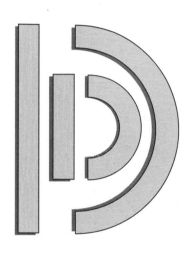

Wood Pieces Set
for Capital Letters

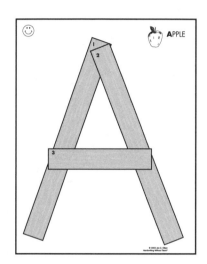

Capital Letter Cards
for Wood Pieces

HWT Mat
for Wood Pieces

HWT Slate Chalkboard

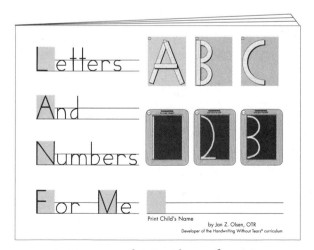

Letters and Numbers for Me
Kindergarten Workbook

by Jan Z. Olsen, OTR

Developer of the Handwriting Without Tears® curriculum

Handwriting Without Tears®
Jan Z. Olsen, OTR

8001 MacArthur Blvd
Cabin John, MD 20818
Phone: 301–263–2700 • Fax: 301–263–2707
www.hwtears.com • JanOlsen@hwtears.com

Handwriting Without Tears Teacher's Guide

Aa Bb Cc Dd Ee Ff Gg Hh Ii Jj Kk Ll Mm Nn
Oo Pp Qq Rr Ss Tt Uu Vv Ww Xx Yy Zz

Welcome

Welcome to the Handwriting Without Tears® method! I'm Jan Olsen, the developer of the program. I'm an occupational therapist and have specialized in handwriting for more than 25 years.

Handwriting Without Tears® (HWT) is a simple, developmentally based curriculum for writing readiness, printing, and cursive. The multisensory lessons teach to all learning styles—visual, auditory, tactile, and kinesthetic. The unique materials and appealing workbooks eliminate problems with letter formation, reversals, legibility, sentence spacing, and cursive connections. Teachers, parents, and children find the program enjoyable, even fun, and the results very satisfying.

It is my goal to make handwriting available to all children as an automatic and natural skill. Children who write well perform better in school, enjoy their classes more, and feel proud of their work.

Introduction

Handwriting Without Tears Teacher's Guide provides unique teaching tips and lesson plans for using the Wood Pieces Set for Capital Letters, the Capital Letter Cards, the HWT Mat and the HWT Slate Chalkboard. These manipulatives develop children's readiness skills. This guide also gives specific teaching tips about the kindergarten student workbook, *Letters and Numbers for Me*.

The lesson plans and teaching tips in this guide will show you how to help your children develop excellent printing habits and skills. You will learn how the HWT letter style, teaching order, workbook design, and unique teaching strategies make printing easier for children. There are suggestions for fun ways to help children with posture, pencil grip, and paper placement. The simple lesson plans make teaching a breeze. Keep the lessons short and fun—you will give your children a great start in handwriting.

Jan Z. Olsen

Handwriting Without Tears® Formation Chart

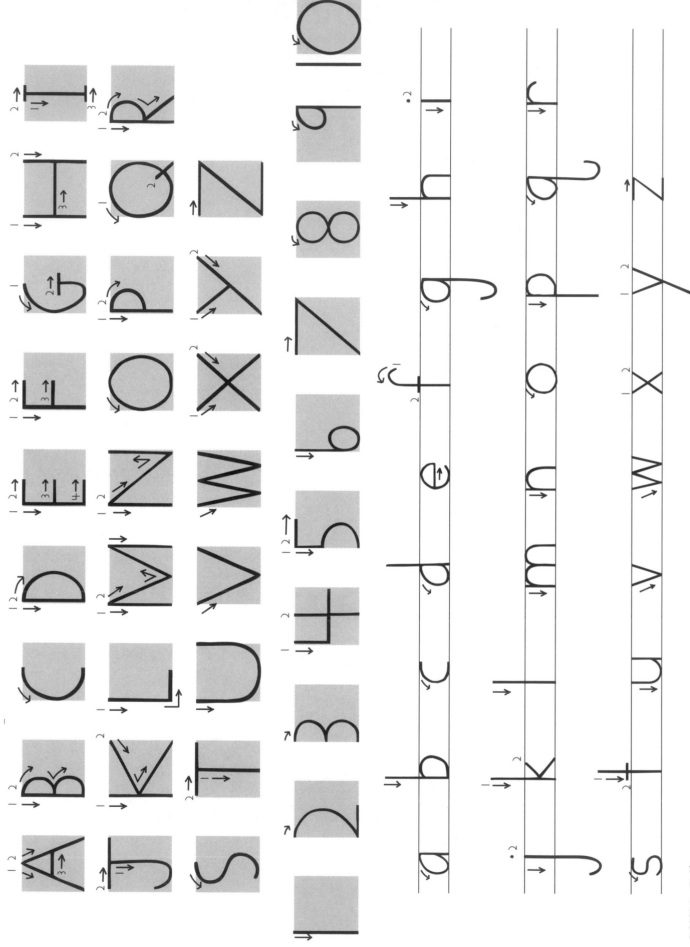

Table of Contents

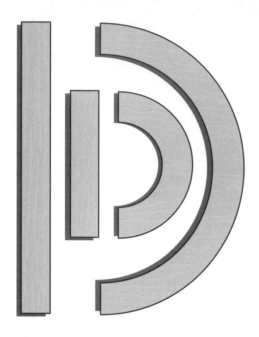

The Wood Pieces Set for Capital Letters includes: 8 big lines, 6 little lines, 6 big curves and 6 little curves.

Through interactive, teacher directed play, children polish, stack, sort and name the pieces. Wood Pieces help children develop their fine motor skills, vocabulary and figure ground discrimination.

Children learn to imitate and follow a teacher's directions. They also learn to hold and move the pieces in various positions, while learning the words that describe these positions.

The Wood Pieces give children a "feel" for how to make capital letters.

Take a Look at the Capital Letter Cards and the HWT Mat

Capital Letter Cards

Building capital letters

Capital Letter Cards are ideal for children who are just learning capitals. The set includes 26 cards. On the front of the card there is an image of a capital letter formed with the wood pieces. Every card has a ☺ in the top left corner to orient the letter right side up. Cards also have a labeled picture to associate with the letter. Children pick up the wood pieces and place them on the card in the correct position and order to form capital letters.

*See full size sample at back of book.

Pre-writing and language skills

The back side of the card has four sets of same and different exercises. The front side teaches the formation of the letter, the back side teaches children to distinguish objects from one another, capitals from capitals, and capitals from lowercase.

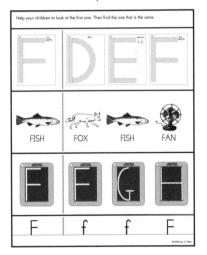

HWT Mat for Wood Pieces

This blue foam mat measures 8½" by 11". In the top left corner is a bright yellow smiley face. By following the teacher's demonstration, children place the wood pieces on the mat to make capital letters. They learn to make all capital letters correctly—right side up, in the correct sequence of pieces, and facing the right way.

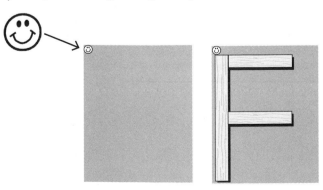

Children use the **Wood Pieces** and **Mat** to learn how to form capital letters correctly.

Great for capitals!

Great for numbers!

The chalkboard is made of real slate, measuring 4" by 6", in a sturdy wood frame. The ☺ at the top left corner orients children and reinforces top to bottom, left to right directionality.

- The slate provides a frame of reference so that children write capitals and numbers.
- The edge of the frame helps children control starting and stopping to make letters a consistent size.
- The slate activities improve children's finger dexterity, helping them to develop a good pencil grip.

"Wet–Dry–Try"

Teacher's Part   **Student's Part**

WET   **DRY**   **TRY**

Our unique Wet–Dry–Try teaching method is a multi-sensory strategy that is really fun for the students and helps them learn the proper formation of capitals and numbers.

- The fun and tactile slate lessons prepare your children for pencil and paper.

4

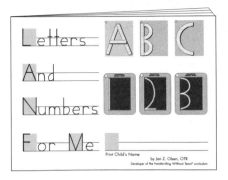

Letters and Numbers for Me (orange cover) is for kindergarten students or older students working at that level. It does not have a grade level on the cover in consideration of older children using the book. Capital letters are taught first, using delightful multisensory strategies. Capital letter lessons prepare students for lowercase. The focus is on correct letter formation and placement. Children learn to print words and simple sentences. Number lessons are near the middle of the book and these pages should be taught before or during arithmetic lessons.

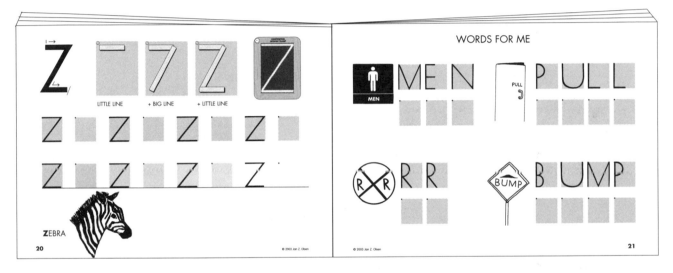

The capital letter pages have huge step-by-step instructions for each new letter. The teacher demonstrates each step and checks to be sure children form letters correctly in the gray blocks.

Word pages show how capitals are used in everyday life. There are also fun games that help children develop correct habits.

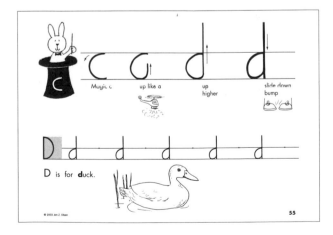

The pages for teaching lowercase letters have huge step-by-step illustrated instructions. The teacher demonstrates each step and the children finger trace the model before they write the letter with a pencil.

Words for Me and Sentences for Me pages are presented throughout the book to help the children master what they have learned.

Tips for You

The tips and lesson plans in this guide will help you be a great handwriting teacher. If you are like most educators, parents or therapists, you've had minimal or no handwriting training. Based on responses from tens of thousands of teacher at our workshops, we know that only ten percent of elementary teachers have received any previous training. Without training, many teachers just pass out workbooks and neglect teaching. We don't want you to do that! Combined with your personal teaching style, our program will enable you to bring the program alive for your students with active and dynamic instruction. Parents, administrators, you, and most importantly the children will be delighted with your students' great success.

Teach a Short, Daily Handwriting Lesson

There are pressures from everywhere to cram more stuff into the instructor's day and it is very difficult. Making time for handwriting, however, will make it easier for you to fit everything else in! Spending a little time everyday with *Handwriting Without Tears*, you will no longer have painfully slow writers, sloppy writers, or children avoiding writing altogether. Further, you won't have to waste time struggling to read your students' work.

Three Stages of Learning

Children learn to write correctly and easily when instructions follow these three developmentally based stages.

Stage 1 – Imitation:
The teacher physically demonstrates how to write B.
The child imitates the teacher to make B.
Think of this analogy—It is easiest to draw a horse when you have someone to show you step-by-step how to do it. You imitate.

Stage 2 – Copying:
There is a model of the letter B on a practice page.
The child copies B by looking at the model of letter B.
Think of this analogy—It is easy to draw a horse when you have a picture of a horse to look at. You copy.

Stage 3 – Independent Writing:
There is no demonstration and there is no model of the letter B. The child writes B independently.
Think of this analogy—It is a challenge to draw a horse when you have to do it from memory. You draw it independently.

Teaching at stage one, with lots of active demonstration makes it so much easier for children to learn. Your dynamic demonstrations will teach to their visual, auditory and kinesthetic learning styles. Once children can imitate correctly, they are ready to copy from the models in the workbooks. Children who can copy well are ready for independent writing. Any time a child is struggling, go back to an easier stage.

Starting at the Top is Important

When you demonstrate, teach your children to start their letters at the top. Try this:
Make 5 lines down.   Make 5 lines, alternating down/up.   Now do it again, very fast.

By starting at the top, you can be both fast and neat. Children who start letters at the bottom are either slow or sloppy. In this guide, you'll learn how to correct bad habits and emphasize good habits with easy and fun techniques.

Kindergarten Teachers

Teaching kindergarten is wonderful. You have:
- Young children whose outlook and habits can be shaped.
- Children who are excited to learn to recognize and write letters and words

Teaching kindergarten is a challenge too. You face:
- Children with different developmental abilities compounded by the significance of age differences for young children.
- Children with very different pre-school and home preparation.

Tips for Your Room

Classroom style
Move chairs and tables so that all children are facing the board when you teach. Avoid children sitting across from each other if possible. They look across and see upside-down printing. Try to make sure that the furniture size is appropriate for the child's size.

Display bright yellow ☺ faces
English is a top to bottom, left to right language. Putting ☺ faces in the top left corners of your doors and boards promotes starting at the top and reading/writing from left to right. It also turns your door into a large teaching tool for arm tracing in the air.

Have a big board space for free use
This is for classroom graffiti. Children watch and learn from each other. Large spaces allow for exploring and associating movement and line/marks.

Provide small pieces of chalk and crayon
Little pieces are perfect for little hands because they require children to use their fingertips correctly. Little pieces prepare the hand for using a good pencil grip. Little bits of crayon are appealing if placed by color in little bowls.

Tips for Lessons

Teach names
Let beginners write their names in all capitals. Gradually show these children the lowercase letters they need. Use the "My Name" page at the back of the workbook.

Compliment your reading curriculum
Because reading and handwriting are different skills, the letter order for reading instruction will not always match the order used for handwriting. This is typically fine. You may introduce some handwriting letters out of sequence if necessary.

Don't even think of journals for beginners
Journal assignments are not for beginners. Avoid journals until your children have learned to write the letters correctly. Otherwise, they'll draw their letters and learn bad habits. Don't worry about the "play writing" they do on their own. That play is minimal and not harmful.

Love those capital letters
Start with capitals because they're easier and familiar! Capitals give little children such a smooth start. Once they know their capitals, the transition to lowercase letters is easy. That's because children begin lower case with letters they know from capitals—c o s v w.

Do posture, paper and pencil preparation before lessons: See pages 30–33 for suggestions to develop good posture, paper placement and pencil grip.

Kindergarten Teachers continued...

Tips for Teaching Children of All Ability Levels

Help children learn to hold a pencil
Continually show and teach children how to place their fingers to hold the pencil correctly. See pages 32 and 33 of this guide for tips.

Keep skilled printers occupied
Tell the children who finish quickly to color the picture. The black and white illustrations and extra space are designed especially for coloring and drawing.

Meet the needs of all children
You can be teaching the same letter to all your children. Some may need to learn that letter with a wood piece lesson, others with the "wet–dry–try" slate activity, and others are ready for the workbook page. You can accommodate individual learning styles and different ability levels.

Say good-bye to bad habits
Are they starting letters at the bottom, or making reversals? Don't despair. HWT has a secret strategy to prevent children from using those bad habits. See the fun, mystery games on page 11 and 57 of the *Letters And Numbers For Me* workbook. Read about this strategy on pages 40–41 and 70 of this guide.

Help children who don't know their letters
There is no need to wait until children recognize their letters to begin this handwriting curriculum. All children can participate fully from the start. They develop letter recognition as they use the program.

Help children who don't speak English
The illustrated step-by-step letter demonstrations require no reading ability for the child to learn how to form the letters. Simple words and picture cues and repeated sentence patterns encourage children to read.

Tips for Involving Parents and Homework

Send home the letter formation chart
Copy the page with capital, number, and lowercase letter formation chart from the back of this Teacher's Guide. Send it home with a note similar to this:

Dear Parents:

We are using the Handwriting Without Tears® curriculum. This chart shows you how to make the letters and numbers. We will be learning the capital letters first. See **www.hwtears.com** for more information about this curriculum. We are excited about helping your child develop good handwriting skills.

Sing "Where Do You Start Your Letter?"
Send your kindergarten students home singing that song. Parents love to hear children sing and parents learn the words too. Parents are the most important teachers, and if parents show children how to make letters correctly; that makes your work much easier. All letters except d and e start at the top.

Avoid "handwriting" homework
Your students' work in class and with *Letters and Numbers for Me* is generally sufficient. If a child needs extra support, give parents suggestions for helping. Such help should take just five minutes per day.

Parents and Homeschoolers

Teaching your own child is delightful. You have:
- More freedom to customize pacing to the child's needs and abilities.
- More ability to provide individual attention.

Teaching your own child is a challenge too. You may face:
- Insecurities about your ability to be an effective instructor.
- Balancing the roles of teacher and parent.

Tips for Lessons

Assure interest and cooperation
Don't go too fast. Parents are often so eager and pleased that they try to get their children to do one more word or one more sentence. Resist the temptation. Keep lessons short (10 to 15 minutes) and have your child practice for only about 5 minutes of that time.

Balance reading and handwriting
Remember that while both are language skills, handwriting requires different fine motor and perceptual skills. When the child's language arts skills are much more advanced than handwriting skills, use other methods (dictation and keyboarding) to get around written work until the printing skills catch up.

Help your child hold the pencil
Preparing the hand for holding a pencil starts very early, long before you'd give a child a pencil. Give your child lots of finger foods. While certain toys aren't safe before age three or so because children will swallow them, food is fine! Picking up small grains of rice, dry cereal, raisins, and small cubes of cheese develops finger dexterity and the open pinch that will be used for pencils later.

I suggest that you closely monitor how your child holds a crayon or marker. Some children actually do pick up and use a crayon correctly very early. But, if your child is holding the crayon with a fisted grip, put the crayons away. It is hard to break bad habits. But, it is easy to break crayons! Break crayons (while your child isn't looking!) and arrange the little bits attractively in small bowls by color, perhaps on a lazy susan to make them appealing. Give your child the writing tools that elicit a good grip. You will notice a developmental change when your child shifts from writing with big arm movements to actual handwriting when the child learns to rest the hand on the paper. Continually show your child how to hold the pencil correctly. Refer to pages 32–33 for additional tips.

Show children how to write their names
Children want to write their names and they usually can if you show them how to write in capitals first. Feel free to teach the letters for your child's name out of workbook order. If your child can write some letters but not others, let her write what she can, and you can complete the remainder. Blank paper is fine, but draw a smiley face at the very top left corner of the paper and start there. Place the pencil at the top of the paper for every letter. You should have your own paper and write each letter stroke by stroke for your child to imitate. Be sure to start at the top. You may use a single bottom line for children who can stop on a line. For children who can't stop, give them a narrow strip of paper to write on. They will use the height of the paper as the height of the letters. (See page 36.)

Teach informally as you go about life
Stuck in a grocery line? Look for letters! Many of the frustrations of everyday life can be turned into pleasant, worthwhile experiences if you look for something around you to share with your child. Books are wonderful, but signs will do when you're out and about.

Tips for Working Together

Your child and your child's teacher need to be comfortable with what you're doing. Sometimes teachers are very loyal to a particular method or system. Try to understand this, but communicate that your primary loyalty is to your child and what works for your child. Most teachers will support parents who approach them with respect and a desire to help.

Therapists and Specialists

Assisting children who have handwriting problems is very satisfying. You have:
- Professional skills and experience to serve the children.
- More ability to provide individual attention.

Assisting children who have handwriting problems is a challenge too. You face:
- Children who are not able to keep up with their peers or their school work.
- Limited time for consultations.

Good handwriting helps children with all school subjects.

Tips for Working with Others

Look at more than the child
As a consultant you'll assess the child but also try to assess the child's learning environment. Ask to see the workbook or handwriting materials that the child is using. Find out what the child's classroom handwriting lessons are like. Check the child's desk, chair and classroom placement. Make suggestions to improve the child's learning environment.

Suggest developmentally appropriate learning experiences
Many young children aren't quite ready for paper/pencil tasks. Those children can be successful with other tasks. They can learn letter recognition and formation with wood pieces and HWT Capital Letter Cards. They can learn letters and numbers on a slate. Instead of producing meaningless, messy papers, they will learn foundation skills for letters and numbers. At the appropriate level you can have even more success by teaching at a slower pace, using the child's preferred sensory learning style, and giving lots of demonstration/imitation lessons.

Achieve continuity when you see students infrequently
Cooperate with the people at school. Talk to parents and volunteers. Share your skills and show others what you do. Consider working with groups to give children more contact time.

Tips for Lessons

Avoid dot to dot letter tracing and other inappropriate tasks
Often children with special needs are given work that is totally inappropriate. A perfect example is the common practice of dot to dot name tracing. Children may trace dots for years and not be able to write their names. Here's why. They're just trying to get from one dot to the next dot. They don't "see" each letter as a whole. For the best results, use developmentally appropriate materials and strategies.

Teach consistent, simple words
The readiness activities teach children the size, shape, and position words. Teachers then use these words consistently when giving directions for making letters. Refer to pages 19–22. Children learn the words so they can understand the directions.

Teach letter names and sounds: Children are excited to learn letter names when they build letters out of the wood pieces. The "Sign In Please!" activity on page 14 encourages children to associate letter names and letter sounds with the names of their classmates.

Letters and Numbers for Me promotes reading
The kindergarten workbook has illustrations designed to promote left to right directionality and visual tracking. The pictures that face sideways are facing to the right.

FISH

C is for **c**ow.

Readiness Made Easy

What makes Handwriting Without Tears® so fun and effective for students and teachers? It is the combination of our letter style, the order in which we teach various skills, the product and workbook designs, and our unique teaching strategies.

We capture each facet of this combination in our "Made Easy" sections in this guide. You are about to start reading Readiness Made Easy and later in this guide you will learn about Capital Letters Made Easy (page 34), Numbers Made Easy (page 50), and finally Lowercase Letters Made Easy (page 57).

HWT Letter Style

HWT uses a simple, vertical style for capitals, lowercase letters, and numbers.

The capital letters are especially easy to learn because they are constructed from just four basic pieces: big lines, little lines, big curves, and little curves.

Teaching Order

Readiness begins with multi-sensory play

Learning to write does not begin with seat-work! Paper-pencil work is out. Learning to write begins with multi-sensory play. Little children learn with all their senses. They are eager, curious and on the move. They need to be actively moving, touching, feeling and manipulating real objects.
HWT activities have children polishing, stacking, sorting, trading, feeling, squeezing, moving, placing, standing, sitting, and shaking hands. Children use the unique HWT materials for both overall readiness and direct preparation for printing capital letters and numbers.

Readiness begins by developing language

Not all children speak English or understand what the teacher says. That's OK! The HWT readiness activities will teach them in a positive, natural way. The activities let all children participate fully regardless of their language ability. HWT is totally accessible!

When the children are playing with the HWT Capital Letter Wood Pieces, the teacher casually calls the pieces by name (big line, little line, big curve and little curve). "I'm collecting the big lines; who has a big line?" Soon the children are picking up the words "big line" as easily as they pick up the pieces. Consistency in naming the pieces gets children ready to follow directions such as "For R, make a big line first."

That's not all. Children hold a wood piece up in the air and say "up in the air." They hold two big curves "apart" and then put them "together." By moving the wood pieces and imitating the teacher they learn words (top-middle-bottom, up-down, over-under, left-right, etc.) for position and direction. Other readiness activities teach children's names, letter names, and letter sounds.

Readiness facilitates social learning

Social behaviors are important for successful learning. HWT readiness actively promotes social and school skills. The "Shake Hands with Me" activity facilitates eye contact and greeting skills. The "Wood Pieces on the Floor" activity encourages cooperative play. The "Sign In" activity gently prepares children to stand in front of a class. Children also learn to watch and imitate the teacher, to do things in order and to follow a structure. This makes children happier and more successful in all learning tasks.

Ready for capital letters!

What's easier, capitals or lowercase letters? Teachers agree that capitals are easier and that's where we begin. It is also smart to start with less. Rather than give little children the overwhelming task of learning 62 symbols (26 capital letters, 26 lowercase letters and 10 basic number symbols), HWT starts with just capitals.

Use developmental principles

Some letters are easier to write (developmentally) than others. Children gradually develop the ability to copy forms in a very predictable order.* This order is shown below.

After examining this developmental order, it is easy to determine which letters are easy and which are hard. Generally, letters that use just vertical and horizontal lines are the easiest, while letters with diagonal lines are difficult. Readiness activities are designed to help children feel at home with vertical and horizontal lines, curves and circles, and diagonal lines. See pages 20–22.

Capital letters are easy

- All are the same height.
- All start at the same place—the top.
- All occupy the same vertical place.
- All are easy to recognize and identify (compare A B D G P Q with a b d g p q).
- They are big, bold, and familiar.

Lowercase letters are more difficult

- Lowercase letters are not the same size.
- Lowercase letters are more difficult to recognize because of subtle differences (a b d g p q).
- Lowercase letters occupy three different vertical positions.

- Lowercase letters start in four different places.

*Gesell, Arnold, and others. *The First Five Years of Life.* New York: Harper and Row. 1940.

Readiness prepares children for symbols

What are reading, writing, and arithmetic? They are skills that use symbols. Letters and numbers are symbols. When children enter school, they are coming to a place where the primary focus is on the mastery of symbols.

Little children have been living in the real world at home. Their experiences at home may lead to some confusion as they make the transition to school and symbols. That's because in the real world, position doesn't affect identity. Children know that grandmother is still grandmother no matter which way she's facing. That's true of people, animals, clothing, food, etc.

When children enter school, they must learn to use symbols. With symbols, there are different rules. Position can and does change identity. Think of the letter "M." Turn it and it's a "W." That's why it's very natural for children to make reversals. They may not realize that with symbols, position is very important. The HWT activities teach children how the letter and number symbols should face.

In the real world, position doesn't matter: they are both dogs.

With symbols, position does matter: only d is for dog!

Product Design

Wood Pieces Set

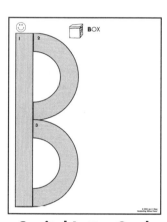

Capital Letter Card

HWT Mat

HWT Slate

HWT has unique "No paper, no pencil" products. They are perfect for developing skills in a playful but carefully structured way. The **Wood Pieces Set for Capital Letters** are everyone's favorite. The 26–piece set has 8 big lines, 6 little lines, 6 big curves and 6 little curves. At first the pieces are used to teach size, shape and position skills. Then wood pieces are used to teach letters on either the **HWT Capital Letter Cards** (26 piece ABC set) or the **HWT Mat**. These two products ensure that children learn to make the letters correctly.

The HWT Capital Letter Cards show a pre-made letter. The child's task is to match and place the real wood pieces on the card. The back of the card has four sets of same and different exercises. This teaches children to distinguish objects, capitals from capitals, and capitals from lowercase. The HWT Mat does not have the pre-made letters. It is a blue mat with a bright yellow ☺ in the top left corner. Both the cards and the mat use a ☺ as a cue for orientation. The teacher always demonstrates first so that children see how to place each piece on the card or the mat.

After making a few letters, children are ready to write, but not on paper. They write on the **HWT Slate Chalkboard** with a tiny piece of chalk (to promote the correct pencil grip). This is real writing. Children make the chalk move in exactly the strokes they will use on paper. They go from writing on the slate to writing on paper with confidence. Slates are used to teach capital letters and numbers.

Unique Teaching Strategies

Sign in Please!

You may remember an old TV show where the guests signed in. This adaptation is fun and develops many ABC skills. Children sign in alphabetically.

Preparation

1. Prepare blackboard with a wide "stop" line near the bottom. (A blackboard is best, but you may use a white board.)
2. Break chalk into small 1/2" pieces to encourage correct pinch.

Directions

1. Teacher prints A.
   - Write A up high, but reachable for children.
   - Teach A and each letter that follows as you write.
   - Use consistent words as you demonstrate (A = big line, big line, and little line).
2. Teacher asks, "Whose name begin with A?" **Adam**!
3. Adam comes to the board and you introduce him saying:
   "This is..... (children say **Adam**)."
   "Adam starts with.....(children say **A**)."
   "In Adam's name, the A makes the sound (children make the **a sound**)."
4. Adam signs in by making a big line down from A. He stops on the line. Continue with each letter. Children sign in alphabetically. David is at the board now.

What Are We Learning?

- **Top to bottom** habit.
- **Stopping** on a line.
- **Names** of capital letters and classmates.
- **Phonics**—Sounds of letters are easy to do with classmates' names.
- **Correct letter formation**—Children learn by watching and hearing the teacher.
- **Big line, little line, big curve, and little curve**—They learn the names for the parts of each letter.
- **Alphabetical order**—Children quickly learn their place in the alphabet. They guess which letter is next and watch to see if they're right. They look for classmates' names too.
- **Left to right** sequencing.
- **Social skills** for school—This is a fun way to learn to listen, be in front of the class, follow directions, and take turns. Children develop poise and a sense of belonging.
- **Pencil grip**—The small pieces of chalk encourage correct grip.
- **Number concepts**—Counting, comparing, and simple charting skills.

Variation: You can change how children sign in to teach other skills.
- Horizontal line skills—Underline letter from left to right.
- Circle skills—Circle the letter by starting at the top with a C stroke.

14

Shake Hands with Me

With this amazing activity children learn right/left discrimination and social skills

Preparation

1. Gather what's needed for the sensory part. Each day uses a different sensory modality—hand lotion, a bowl of water, a rubber stamp, scents or flavoring, etc.
2. Assemble the children in a group.

Directions

1. Shake hands with each child. Smile, make eye contact and say a personal greeting, "Good morning, Patrick!" Gently encourage a returned smile, eye contact and greeting.
2. Immediately give sensation to the hand you shook and say:
   This is your right hand. I'm going to:
   - Rub your hand. It's warm now. Make a fist and keep it warm.
   - Dip your fingers in water. Watch them drip!
   - Stamp your hand with a smiley face. Look at that!
   - Dab some peppermint on your finger. Smell it.
   - Put lotion on your thumb pad and index finger. Rub them together.
3. Now have all the children raise their right hands and say:
   - This is my right hand.
   - I shake hands with my right hand.
   - (For USA only!) I say the Pledge of Allegiance with my right hand.
   - (Optional: Name the sensory experience.) My right hand was warm.

What Are We Learning?

- Social skills for meeting and greeting
- To automatically use the right hand for shaking hands (and the pledge).
- Which hand is the right hand
- A sense of directionality on our own bodies.

Tips

- Use daily for a week or two and then as desired. Children learn this quickly.
- The secret to this activity (It really works!) is that it teaches just the right hand.
- Do not teach the left. If they know the right hand, it's easy. What's left is left.
- Don't worry. This is appropriate for left handed children. All children, whether right or left handed, should shake hands and say the pledge with the right hand.
- Handwriting Without Tears® is a very left hand friendly curriculum. This activity is not trying to promote right-handedness. It is simply to teach social skills and right/left discrimination.

An Easel to Share

Give your children lots of free blackboard space and, if you can, give them a huge easel to share. Use an old bi-fold door and fasten it to a table. The illustration shows you how it should look. The advantage of such an easel is that several children can use it at the same time. They learn from watching each other move and make marks. Just roll out the paper and let them scribble and start to draw. With such an easel children can walk along and drag a horizontal line or swing an arm around to get a circular stroke. Give them little pieces of crayon or chalk to use and they'll develop a fingertip pinch for holding a pencil.

Sing "Where Do You Start Your Letters?"

The inside back cover of *Letters and Numbers for Me* has a song. You know the tune; it's "If You're Happy and You Know It." But the words are different. They say, "Where Do You Start Your Letters?" Sing this song so often that your children will sing it at home and in the family car. Here's why. The parents listen. Parents are a child's first and most important teachers. It's parents who show children how to make their letters. With this song, you are actually teaching the parents how to help their children. If they know that letters should start at the top, parents will model that for their children. Starting at the top is such an important skill. Children who start letters at the top learn to print automatically with speed and neatness. Children who vary where they start letters end up thinking about how to write each letter rather than writing automatically.

Use this song when you're teaching or reviewing PRINTED CAPITALS.

Tune: "If You're Happy and You Know It"

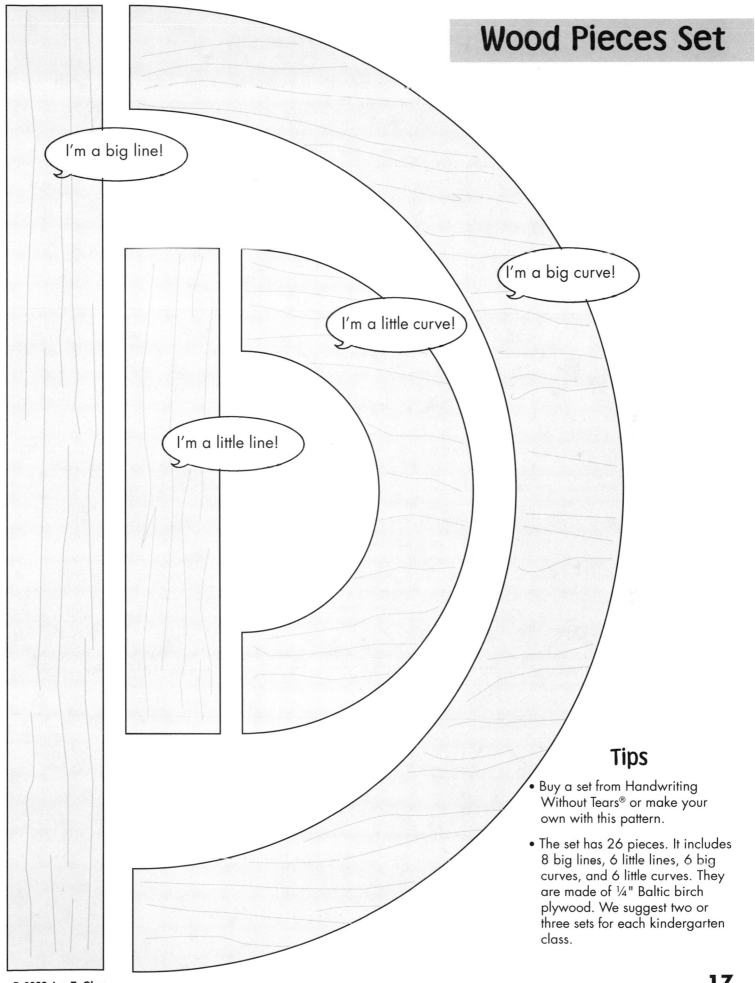

Wood Pieces Set

Tips

- Buy a set from Handwriting Without Tears® or make your own with this pattern.

- The set has 26 pieces. It includes 8 big lines, 6 little lines, 6 big curves, and 6 little curves. They are made of ¼" Baltic birch plywood. We suggest two or three sets for each kindergarten class.

Wood Pieces on the Floor

Key Point: Working with the Wood Pieces Set is a fun and relaxed way to teach children the concepts of and the words to describe size and shape. This activity prepares children for making capital letters.

Show children how to polish, stack, and sort the wood pieces. This is a friendly, relaxed, and worthwhile activity that children love. Talk about the pieces. Gradually, the children will pick up the important words (big line, little line, big curve, little curve) along with the pieces!

"You have a big curve. I have a big curve. We picked the same pieces."
"You have a big line. I have a big curve. Do you want to trade?"
"Let's polish lines. Do you want to polish a big line or a little line?"
"It's time to collect the wood pieces. Who has a big line?"

What Are We Learning?
- Size and Shape—Children can feel and see the difference between big and little, line and curve.
- Vocabulary—Children begin to use consistent words (big line, little line, big curve, little curve) to describe the pieces.
- Social Skills—Children learn to work together, share, trade, pay attention, and imitate.
- Bi-lateral Hand Skills—Using one hand to hold a piece while the other rubs helps develop a child's fine motor skills.
- Visual Skills—Children begin to see the differences in size and shapes.
- Figure Ground Discrimination—Finding a particular piece in an assortment of scattered pieces.

Wood Pieces in the Bag

Key Point: Children learn with a sense of touch.

Prepare for this activity by filling a bag with assorted HWT Capital Letter Wood Pieces. Hold the bag. Child reaches inside, feels one piece, guesses which piece it is, and then takes it out.

What Are We Learning?
- Tactile Discrimination of Size and Shape—Children feel the characteristics of the piece they are touching.
- Vocabulary—Children use consistent words to describe size and shape (big line, little line, big curve, and little curve).
- Fine Motor Skills—Reaching in the bag and manipulating the piece with one hand develops manipulative skills.
- Taking Turns—Waiting for a turn.

Tips
- You can easily grade this activity just by what you put in the bag. For very young children or children with special needs, put in just two different shapes.
- Make it extra fun by adding objects too, like a ping-pong ball or a spoon. Children will use words that describe the size and shape of these objects.

Position in Space and Body Parts with Wood Pieces

Key Point: Children learn position words and placement skills with wood pieces.

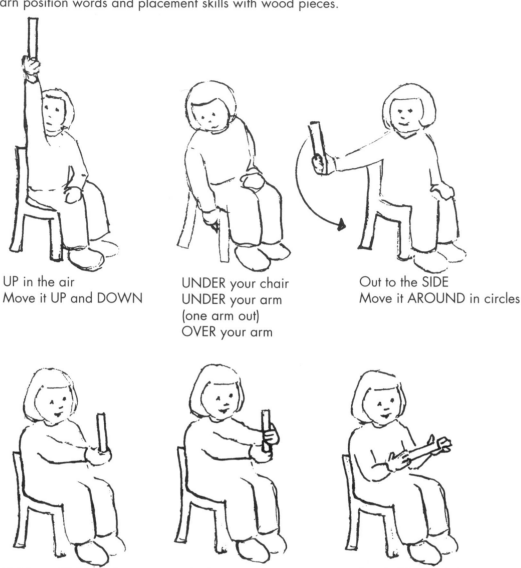

UP in the air
Move it UP and DOWN

UNDER your chair
UNDER your arm
(one arm out)
OVER your arm

Out to the SIDE
Move it AROUND in circles

Hold it in FRONT of you
Hold it at the BOTTOM
It's VERTICAL

Climb UP and DOWN
Hold it at the BOTTOM,
MIDDLE, TOP

Say HORIZONTAL
Move it SIDE to SIDE

Prepare for this activity by passing a big line or little line to each student. Say the name of each position or body part as you demonstrate. Have children say it too.

What Are We Learning?
- Imitating—Children learn to watch and follow the teacher.
- Positioning—Children learn to hold and move the pieces in various positions.
  They learn the words that describe position.

Tips
- Teach other position words such as: BEHIND my back, BETWEEN my fingers, BESIDE me, THROUGH my arm (put hand on hip first), ON my lap.
- When teaching TOP, BOTTOM, MIDDLE use a big line. Teacher holds big line with just one hand at the BOTTOM, then changes hands and positions, naming the position each time. Children imitate.
- Teach body parts by naming each body part as you touch it with a wood piece.

20

Vertical, Horizontal, and Diagonal

Key Point: By imitating you, children learn position and placement skills and words. Prepare by giving each child the pieces to be used.

Hold two big lines in one hand.

Open them! Hold them out. Say, "Voila! It's a V." (Guide child in finger tracing the V.)

Hold two big lines end to end diagonally. Move and say, "Diagonal, diagonal."

Make a big line stand up. Make it "walk" on your arm.

Now it's tired. Make it lie down.

One big line is standing up. One little line across the top. It's a T.

Hold one big line in each hand.

Put them together at the top. Looks like a teepee or the start of the A.

Together at the middle— It's an X! X marks the spot!

What Are We Learning?
- Vertical and Horizontal—Moving the pieces in vertical and horizontal positions prepares children to make capitals E F H I L T.
- Diagonal—Moving the lines diagonally prepares children to make capitals A K M N R V W X Y Z. They make V and X and the beginning of A.

Tips
- Do a tapping activity with two big lines held like an X. Teacher taps and students wait to tap until teacher says, "Your turn!" Use just two taps (1–2) until children learn to listen and wait. When they know how to do this, vary the number or rhythm of taps.
- Encourage children to speak with you. The words—vertical, horizontal and diagonal are fun to say with the motions.

Curves and Circles

Key Points: By imitating you, children learn to associate shapes with movement.

APART
Hold the big curves apart.

TOGETHER
Bring them together.

Say "O" or "Zeeeero"
Hold them up to your face.
Make circles in the air now.

RAINBOW—hold a big curve up.
Sing "Somewhere Over the Rainbow." Hold
the big curve with one hand and then with the
other hand, make big curve motions in the air.

SMILE
Hold big curve up to face.
Make smiles in the air.

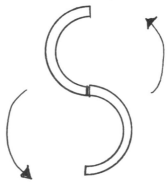

SQUIGGLE—WIGGLE
Hold curves with just one end touching.
Move them alternately up or down.

What Are We Learning?

- Capitals with Curves—Moving and placing the curves prepares children to write the capitals with curves: B C D G J O P Q R S.
- Circle—Children learn that this symbol O can be a shape (circle), a letter (O) and a number (O).
- To Associate Movement with Shape—Moving the arm in an arc or circle prepares children for writing curves and circles.

22

Capitals with Letter Cards

Key Points: Teach children how to place wood pieces on the cards. Do one to three capitals each session. Use this lesson plan for F as a general guide.

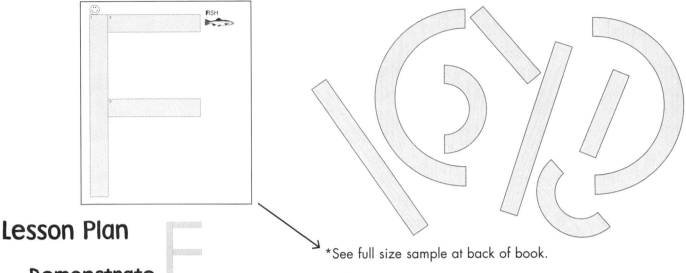

*See full size sample at back of book.

Lesson Plan

Demonstrate
- Place F card in front of child.
- Point to the letter card. Say, "This is F. F starts at the ☺. This word is FISH. FISH begins with F."
- Describe each step as you place the wood pieces on the F. "I'm getting a big line to start F. I'm putting the big line right here, under the ☺. Now, I'm getting a little line to put at the top. There it is. Now, I'm getting another little line to put at the middle. I made F."
- Remove the pieces.

Teach
- When working with a group of children, each child will be making a different letter. Supervise to be sure the pieces are placed in the correct order. Help the children notice the number "1" on the card and then select and place that piece. Follow the numbers to complete each letter correctly.
- When working individually, you may teach planning skills by having the child gather the needed pieces first. Ask, "What do you need to make F? First, you need…a big line. How many? One! Get one big line. Then you need…a little line. How many? Two! Get two little lines. You're ready."

What Are We Learning?
- Letter name for F, associating FISH with F and F sound
- To find the wood pieces for F (1 big line, 2 little lines)
- To place the wood pieces correctly (vertical and horizontal)
- To make the letter F in the correct sequence of steps

Tips
- By spreading out the pieces randomly, you provide a figure-ground activity. Choosing the correct piece (figure) from the assortment (ground) develops visual discrimination.
- Placing each piece requires fine motor control and spatial (position) awareness. You may assist by placing the piece beside the card the way it will be used. Or you may place the piece, take it away and then let the child try.
- Use cards to encourage alphabet awareness. Give each child a card. Have children hold the cards up as the letters are called. Or have children line up alphabetically as the letters are called out.

Pre-Writing and Language Skills with Letter Cards

Key Points: This side of the card has four beginning activities to teach letter awareness and same/different discrimination. Use this lesson plan for F as a general guide.

Lesson Plan

Demonstrate Finding the One that Matches

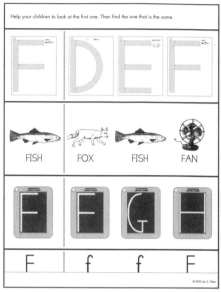

Row 1. Capital letters made with wood pieces
Show children how to point to the first letter. Then demonstrate pointing to each letter in turn; looking for the one that matches. For example:
Show the card. Say, "This page is about the letter F."
Point to F. Say, "The first letter is F. Let's find another F."

Point to D. Ask, "Is this F?...No, no, no. This is D. D is different."
Point to E. Ask, "Is this F?...No, no, no. This is E. E is different."
Point to F. Ask, "Is this F?...Yes! This is F. It is the same letter."

Row 2. Pictures/words that begin with the same capital letter
Show children how to point to the first picture/word. Then demonstrate pointing to each picture/word in turn; looking for the one that matches.
Point to FISH. Say, "This is a fish. FISH starts with F. Let's find another fish."

*See full size sample at back of book.

Point to FOX. Ask, "Is this a FISH? No, no, no. This is a FOX."
Point to FISH. Ask, "Is this a FISH? Yes! This is a FISH. It matches."
Point to FAN. Ask, "Is this a FISH? No, no, no. This is a FAN."

Row 3. Capital letters made with chalk on slates
Find the capital letter that matches the first one.

Row 4. Printed capital and lowercase letters
Find the capital letter that matches the first one.

What Are We Learning?
- Letter name for F and f
- Associating F with the FOX, FISH, FAN, and the F sound
- Same/different concept
- Important habits: Using a page right side up, from top to bottom and left to right
- Difference between capital F and lowercase f

Tips
- For children who don't know letters, just do the activity as if you're reading to the child. Encourage participation by following the child's lead.
- Avoid saying "a" or "an" before a letter name. It's confusing to hear "This is a B." Simply say, "This is B."
- Say "Yes!" enthusiastically and nod your head. Or say "No, no, no" in a cheerful way (like refusing dessert) and shake your head. Children will imitate this.
- The pictures promote left to right directionality. See how they face! Move your finger across each row from left to right and encourage children to imitate this.

Capitals with HWT Mat

Key Points: Teach children how to make capital letters on the HWT MAT. Unlike the cards, the mat does not have a letter printed on it. It is simply a bright blue fabric mat (like a mouse pad) with a yellow ☺ in the top left corner.

Lesson Plan

Demonstrate F

Show the children how to form the letter piece by piece. Teach in a top-to-bottom, left-to-right order. To see the order for any letter, look in *Letters and Numbers for Me*.

Teacher Demonstrates and Student Imitates Piece by Piece

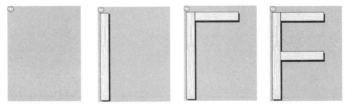

Teach

- When demonstrating, make sure that you make the letter so that it looks right side up from the children's point of view.

What Are We Learning?

- Letter name for F. (Children like letters they can make.)
- To find the wood pieces for F (one big line and two little lines.)
- To make the letter F right side up.
- To place the wood pieces correctly so F is not reversed.
- To make the letter F in the correct sequence of steps.

Tip

- After success with the mat, teach students with the HWT slate.

HWT Slate Chalkboard

Lesson Plan

Demonstrate F
- Put chalk in the starting corner ☺.
- Big line down.
- Frog Jump back up to the starting corner.
- Little line.
- Little line.

Teach on the Slate
Your teaching will vary according to the number of children and slates.
When teacher and students each have a slate:
1. Teacher demonstrates the first step, saying, "I put the chalk in the starting corner."
2. Students imitate that and continue to imitate step by step on their own slates.

When teacher and student share one slate:
1. Teacher demonstrates all steps.
2. Child finger traces the teacher's F. Turn slate over.
3. Teacher says the directions for each step while child makes F.

Tips
- The ☺ is the cue to the top. In a large class students are happy to check each other to be sure all the slates are right side up.
- The ☺ prevents reversals. Children start F E D P B R N K L with a big line down from ☺. The big line is along the left edge so the next part of the letter will always be on the right side.
- The wood frame gives children an edge so that their chalk lines are neat and straight. Their letters are uniform in size and shape.
- The frame and ☺ give children a frame of reference. They can think about the slate and it will help them remember how to make letters.

Evaluate
- If there is difficulty remembering or forming the letter:
  Use the Wet–Dry–Try strategy described on the next page.
- If students have incorrect habits for making capital letters:
  Play the Mystery Letter Game (page 40–41 of this guide) to encourage the top to bottom habit and to correct reversals.

Capitals with HWT Slate

Key Points: The Wet–Dry–Try method is a sensory strategy to teach the strokes for capital letters. Wet–Dry–Try appeals to all learning styles (visual, auditory, tactile, and kinesthetic) and it is lots of fun.

Teacher's Part

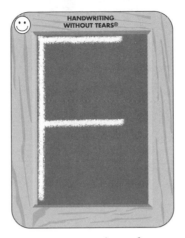

Demonstrate correct letter formation.

Student's Part

WET	**DRY**	**TRY**
Wet tiny sponge. Squeeze out. With damp sponge, trace over the letter like the teacher demonstrated. Wet index finger. Trace letter again with your wet finger.	Use a small piece of paper towel to trace the letter dry. Repeat two or three times.	Now, try writing the letter with a small piece of chalk.

Tips

- Use consistent words to describe the strokes (big line, little line, big curve, little curve).
- Use very small pieces of sponge and chalk—this helps develop the pencil grip.
- Squeeze the sponge well or the letter will be too wet.
- This works best one-on-one or in centers with five or fewer students.
- To use this activity with the whole class you must pre-mark each student slate with the capital letter (so they have a correct model to wet) and then demonstrate once for everyone.

Numbers with the HWT Slate

Key Points: The Wet–Dry–Try method is a sensory strategy to help children learn numbers without reversals. This teaching method works for all learning styles (visual, auditory, tactile, and kinesthetic) and is lots of fun.

Teacher's Part

Demonstrate correct number formation.

Student's Part

WET

Wet tiny sponge. Squeeze out. With damp sponge, trace over the number like the teacher demonstrated. Wet index finger. Trace number again with your wet finger.

DRY

Use a small piece of paper towel to trace the number dry. Repeat two or three times.

TRY

Now, try writing the number with a small piece of chalk.

Tips

- Use very small pieces of sponge and chalk—this helps develop the pencil grip.
- Squeeze the sponge well or the number will be too wet.
- This works best one-on-one or in centers with five or fewer students.
- To use this activity with the whole class you must pre-mark each student slate with the number (so they have a correct model to wet) and then demonstrate once for everyone.

Preparing for Paper and Pencil

1. **READY** Your Room—Simple room preparations will enhance your effectiveness.

2. **SET** Your Children Up—Fun strategies will promote good posture, paper placement, and pencil grip.

3. **GO** for It! Let the teaching begin.

Prepare Your Room

Places everybody! — Classroom style
Sometimes the most obvious things are overlooked. Children need to face the board when you demonstrate. That means standard classroom style. It's not just a matter of vision either. If they are facing you, they'll hear more clearly. That's because ears are shaped to catch sound. When children face you, their ears are in the best position to hear you. This is so simple and so amazing. Even if you need to have the children move the desks, do it! They will see, hear, and pay attention better.

Keep board space clear
You need lots of room to demonstrate letters, words, and sentences. Resist any temptation to use the board as a bulletin board.

Display the alphabet above the board and on desks
The HWT Aa Bb Cc Print Display Cards are plain and suitable for all grades. The letters are the same as the ones you're teaching. Many teachers also like to give each child one of the HWT Alphabet Desk Strips for easy reference.

Furniture size
Does the furniture fit? The right size and style chair and desk affect school performance. Children don't come in a standard size! One size chair will not fit every child. Check that every child can sit with feet flat on the floor and arms resting comfortably on the desk.

When teaching one-on-one
Be sure to place the right-handed child on your right side. Place the left-handed child on your left side. That way you'll be able to clearly see how the child is writing. When you demonstrate be sure that your hand doesn't hide what you're writing.

Good Posture Can Be Fun

Arms and hands
Here are some warm-ups that children enjoy.

Push palms

Pull hands

Hug yourself tightly

Total posture—Stomp!
Stomping is fun and really works! Sit down and show the children how to stomp their feet and wave their arms in the air. Have them shout, "Na, na, naaah, na, na, naaah," with you while waving and stomping. Nothing's better for getting them to sit correctly. Their feet will be on the floor and parallel in front of them. The arm movements make their trunks straight. The noise and chaos lets them release energy, but it's totally under your control. When you have them stop stomping, they'll have good posture and be ready to pay attention. Use stomping a few times a day.

Head and shoulders
Do this anytime you find your children sagging.

Raise shoulders up

Pull shoulders back

Let them down

Place the Paper

Where's the paper? Most children naturally move a bowl of ice cream to be right in front of them. But, they may lean way over in awkward positions to write. So you need to teach them to place the paper.

Left-handed:

Right-handed:

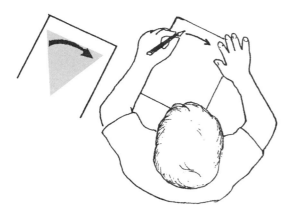
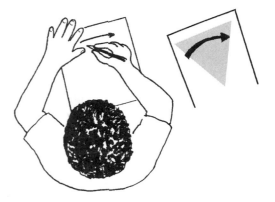

Beginners who are learning to print letters and words should place the paper straight in front of them. Children who are able to print sentences across the page should place the paper at a slight angle to follow the natural arc of the writing hand.

The correct way to tilt the paper is easy to remember (see illustration). For right-handed children, put the right corner higher; for left-handed, the left corner is higher. The writing hand is below the line of writing. This encourages the correct neutral wrist position.

Helping Hand

Where is the "helping hand"—the hand that isn't holding the pencil? I've seen helping hands in laps, twirling hair, or propping up foreheads. So have you! You can nag the child but you'll get better results if you talk directly to the hand! Try it! Take the child's helping hand in yours and pretend to talk to that hand.

Name the helping hand. For example: You have a student named John. Ask John what other name he likes that starts with J. If John says "Jeremy," tell him that you are going to name his helping hand "Jeremy." Have a little talk with "Jeremy" (the helping hand). Tell "Jeremy" that he's supposed to help by holding the paper. Say that John is working really hard on his handwriting, but he needs "Jeremy's" help. Show "Jeremy" where he's supposed to be. Tell John that he might have to remind "Jeremy" about his job.

Kids think this is a hoot. They don't get embarrassed because it's the helping hand, not them, who's being corrected. It's not John who needs to improve, it's "Jeremy." This is a face-saving but effective reminder. One teacher in Wyoming had all her students name their helping hands and even gave them little rings with eyes to wear on the helping hands. The children thought it was fun to tell the helping hand what to do.

Flat fingers please! A flat (but not stiff) helping hand promotes relaxed writing. Put your hand flat on a table and try to feel tension—there isn't any. Make a fist and feel the tension! Children can get uptight while writing, but a flat helping hand decreases tension.

Hold the Pencil

You can put an end to awkward or even fisted pencil grips. Using these tips, your students will hold the pencil with the right combination of mobility and control. Children are "plastic"—they can be molded gently into good habits. These make it easy and fun for children to learn a correct pencil grip.

A-OK
Teach children how to hold the pencil correctly. This is the A-OK way to help children.
The pencil is pinched between the thumb pad and the index finger pad. The pencil rests on the middle finger.

Right-handed:

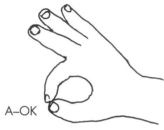 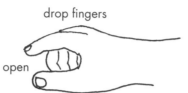 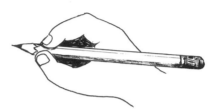

A–OK   drop fingers / open

1. Make the A-OK sign.	**2.** Drop the fingers. Open the A-OK.	**3.** Pinch the pencil.

Left-handed:

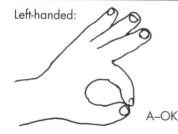 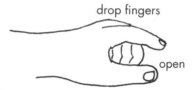 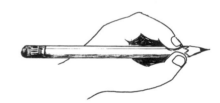

A–OK   drop fingers / open

Alternate Grip
A good alternate grip is a pinch with the thumb and two fingers. The pencil rests on the ring finger.

Left-handed: Right-handed:

Flip the Pencil Trick
Here is another method. It is a trick that someone (in Buffalo, I think) showed me and I've found it so effective and so much fun I've been sharing it ever since. Children like to do it and it puts the pencil in the correct position. (Illustrated for right-handed students.)

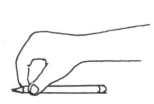 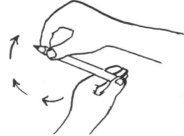 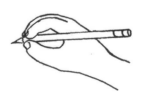

Place pencil on table pointing away from you. Pinch pencil and pick it up. Pinch the pencil where you should hold it—on the paint where the paint meets the wood.

Hold the eraser and twirl it around.

Voila!

Teach the correct pencil grip in three easy steps

This step-by-step technique is a great way to develop a correct pencil grip or to fix awkward ones. The trick is that you don't teach the grip and writing with the grip in the same teaching session. Separate the teaching into these three stages and you will be impressed with how easy the correct grip becomes.

Pick up—Have the child pick up the pencil and hold it in the air with the fingers and thumb correctly placed. Help position the child's fingers if necessary. Tell your students, "Wow that is a perfect pencil grip. Now make a few circles in the air with that perfect pencil grip." Don't let the students write on paper. Just have them pick the pencil up correctly, wave it in the air and gently drop it down. Do this for a few days, until the students can automatically pick up and hold the pencil correctly.

Scribble-wiggle—Give each student a piece of paper with a dot (about three times the size of a period) in the center of the paper. Have the students pick up the pencil, hold it correctly, and put the pencil point on the dot. The little finger side of the "pencil hand" rests on the paper. The child makes wiggly marks through and around the dot without lifting the pencil or hand. (The "helping hand" is flat and holds the paper.) The advantage of this step is that children develop their pencil grip and finger control without being critical of how the writing looks.

Write—Have each student pick up the pencil, hold it correctly and write the first letter of his or her name. Add letters until the children can write their names easily with the correct grip. This will get your students off to a wonderful start. When helping students with poor pencil grips, only insist that they use their new correct grip for writing their names. This will give them frequent practice with the new correct grip. Then slowly build the amount of work that they must do with the new correct grip.

Using pencil grips

If a child continues to have difficulty holding the pencil, there are a variety of grips available at school supply stores, art/stationery stores and catalogs. Their usefulness varies from grip to grip and child to child. Experiment with them and use them only if they make it easier for the child to hold the pencil correctly.

Rubber band trick

Check the angle of the pencil. If it's standing straight up, the pencil will be hard to hold and will cause tension in the fingertips. Put a rubber band around child's wrist. Loop another rubber band to the first one. Pull the loop over to catch the pencil eraser. This may keep the pencil pulled back at the correct angle. If so, you may make or buy a more comfortable version that uses pony tail holders.

Pencil driving tip

Name the fingers: The thumb is the "Dad," the index finger is the "Mom." The remaining fingers are the child and any brothers, sisters, friends, or pets. (Use driver and passenger names to suit child's family.) Say the pencil is the car. Just like in a real car, Dad and Mom sit in front and the kids, friends, or pets sit in back. For safe driving,

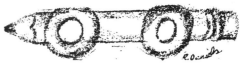

Dad and Mom face forward (toward the point of the pencil). Dad shouldn't sit on Mom's lap (thumb on top of index finger) and Mom shouldn't sit on Dad's lap (index finger on top of thumb)! If children use an overlapping or tucked-in thumb, remind them that no one can sit on anyone's lap while driving! This is a summary of a tip from Betsy Daniels, COTA/L, and Christine Bradshaw, OTR/L. Betsy's daughter did the illustration (copyrighted and used with permission).

Capital Letters Made Easy

The readiness activities have prepared your children for success with capital letters. Now, they're ready to begin *Letters and Numbers for Me*. The workbook begins with capital letter lessons. On the next few pages, see how the HWT letters style, teaching order, workbook design and unique teaching strategies all work together to make learning easy.

HWT Letter Style

ABCDEFGHIJKLMNOPQRSTUVWXYZ

HWT uses a simple, vertical style of printing. Four basic shapes are used to write all of the HWT capital letters. The children already know the four basic shapes for capitals—**big line, little line, big curve, and little curve**—from the HWT wood pieces.

Teaching Order

Teachers may vary the order. Teach a child the letters in his or her name first. If a child has difficulty with diagonal lines (developmentally difficult), save letters with diagonals until later. The developmental sequence is: vertical line, horizontal line, circle, cross, square, and triangle. For capitals, the teaching order is determined by where the letters start and how they are made. Letters that start with the same stroke or in the same place are grouped together.

Frog Jump Capitals

These are the Frog Jump Capitals. They start in the starting corner with a big line down, and then frog jump back to the starting corner to complete the letter.

Starting Corner Capitals

H, K, and L start in the starting corner with a big line down.

U, V, W, X, Y, and Z start in the starting corner but then use different strokes to finish the letter.

Center Starters

C, O, Q, and G start with a "Magic C" stroke.

S, A, I, T, and J start at the top center but then use different strokes to finish the letter.

Workbook Design

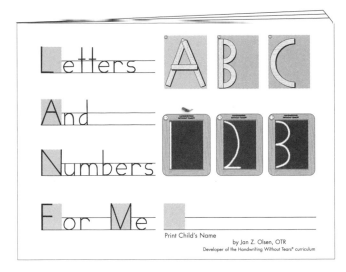

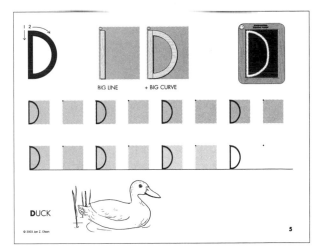

A big, bold letter to finger trace

Writing is the trace of movement. Before the child moves a pencil, the child should finger trace. Finger tracing a big model prepares the child and assures the teacher that the child will be making the letter correctly.

Child-friendly, consistent terminology

Letters and Numbers for Me uses the "wood piece" words "BIG LINE, LITTLE LINE, BIG CURVE or LITTLE CURVE to remind children how to make the letter. The illustrations and wood piece words show the letter being made step by step.

Slate and gray blocks

Children learn the strokes for writing capitals on the slate. Then they use the same strokes with pencil on the gray blocks. The workbook illustration shows the new letter as it looks on the slate. Gray blocks are "pictures" of the slate. Children write with pencil on the gray blocks the same way they wrote with chalk on the slate. A dot on the gray blocks shows children exactly where to put the pencil.

Left (and right) hand friendly

The typical problem for left handed children is that they can't see what they're supposed to copy; it's hidden under their hand. That's never a problem with HWT. By presenting a model in every other gray block, there is always a model in clear view. The left-handed child simply looks to the right when copying.

A better way to practice

In books where children copy a whole line of letters, the letters get progressively worse because they're copying from their own copies. Children get better results if they practice with a model for each copy. The workbook has a model letter in every other gray block, and children write just one letter beside the model. The result is better letters.

Coloring and left to right directionality

In a typical kindergarten class, there is a big range in ability. At five years of age, a few months makes a huge difference. The workbook pages are designed to help you with all your children. Tell the children who complete the letters easily to color the picture. Tell them to draw other things that start with that letter. So, while you're helping a slower child make letters, another child is coloring the fish on the F page and getting ready to draw faces and flowers. The workbook illustrations are designed to promote left to right directionality and visual tracking. The pictures that face sideways always face to the right.

Unique Teaching Strategies

"Wet–Dry–Try" with the HWT Slate

Teaching capitals is fun and reversal proof if you use the HWT Slate Chalkboard. Use this as a preview for children who need a little extra help. See page 27 for directions. This strategy helps children learn to hold the pencil correctly and it prepares them to:.

- Start the capital letter at the top
- Use the correct sequence of strokes.
- Place the capital correctly (no reversal).

Do "Air Letters" with a ☺

Big air writing is good, but you want to be sure that letters are correctly oriented. Put a ☺ in the top left corner of your board. Have the children stand, and face the board and point to the ☺ . Then teach "Frog Jump Capital Letters – F E D P B R N M" in the air. They visualize the first big line on the left edge of the board and the next part will be on the right side. Use the ☺ for these Starting Corner Letters – H K L U V W X Y Z" too.

Demonstrate New Letters

Always demonstrate the new letter by writing in the child's workbook while the child watches. Talk through each step. Seeing how you move and hearing your words gives every child an advantage. The next step is equally important. Watch the child try. Want to give some children extra help? Have them wait and watch you teach one or two others first. By seeing your demonstration more than once, the slower/younger children have a better chance of getting it right. Vary this so they never notice. If it's a very easy letter or one you know a child can do, let them go first.

Write Words on Paper Strips

Writing words on paper strips helps your struggling beginners. Perhaps you have a child who just can't manage the workbook pages, or has difficulty with letter formation or controlling starting and stopping. Try this strategy. Use two strips, one for you and one for the child. Both strips are placed in front of the child, one above the other. The teacher's demonstrates on the top strip. The child imitates, letter by letter, stroke by stroke, until a simple word is complete. The paper itself controls the size of the letters and may be adjusted to the individual. Control in starting is simply putting the pencil near the top of the paper. Control in stopping is just stopping before the pencil marks the table. Letter skills are learned by direct imitation with close teacher supervision.

Teaching
FROG JUMP CAPITALS

Key Points: The Frog Jump Capitals, F E D P B R N M, all begin in the starting corner with a big line down, then frog jump back to the starting corner for the next part of the letter. Use the lesson plan for F as a general guide for all Frog Jump Capitals, F E D P B R N M.

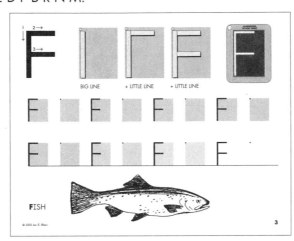

BIG LINE   + LITTLE LINE   + LITTLE LINE

FISH

Lesson Plan

Demonstrate F

Show children how to make F on the HWT Slate Chalkboard or in the workbook. Say the step-by-step directions as you demonstrate. "Start in the starting corner— big line down—frog jump back to the starting corner—little line across the top— little line across the middle."

Teach in workbook

1. At the top of the page:
- Find and finger trace the big, bold F. Follow the arrows, saying the step-by-step directions.
- Review the pictures of making F with the HWT Capital Letter Wood Pieces.
- Finger trace the F on the picture of the slate.

2. In the gray blocks:
- Find F in the gray block.
- Copy F. Put your pencil on the dot (starting corner)—big line down—frog jump to the starting corner—little line across top—little line across middle.
- Complete the first row of gray blocks. Save the second row for tomorrow.

3. At the bottom of the page:
- Find F in FISH.
- Color the fish. Extra: Name words that start with F. Draw a FLOWER or a FACE.

Tips
- Don't worry if the little lines go all the way across or not. It doesn't matter.
- We suggest that left-handed children also make the little lines of F from left to right.
- Watch the children as they form the letter in the gray block.
- Tomorrow, review F before introducing E.

Evaluate
- If there are problems finding the middle for the second little line across:
  Don't worry if it is a little high or low. What is important is the correct sequence of strokes.

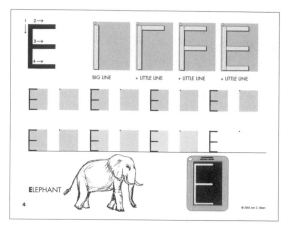

Teaching E

- Put your pencil on the dot (starting corner)—big line down—frog jump to the starting corner—little line across top, middle, and bottom.
- Don't worry if the little lines go all the way across or not. It doesn't matter.
- We suggest that left-handed children also make the little lines of E from left to right.
- Tomorrow, review E before introducing D.

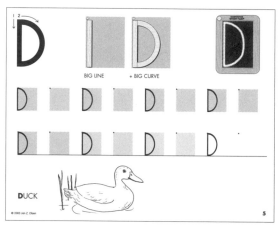

Teaching D

- Put your pencil on the dot (starting corner)—big line down—frog jump to the starting corner—big curve to the bottom corner.
- Don't worry if D is skinny or fat as long as it is made correctly.
- Tomorrow, review D before introducing P.

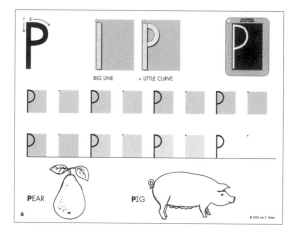

Teaching P

- Put your pencil on the dot (starting corner)—big line down—frog jump to the starting corner—little curve to the middle.
- Hitting the exact middle isn't important, but P must use a little curve and be different from D.
- Tomorrow, review P before introducing B.

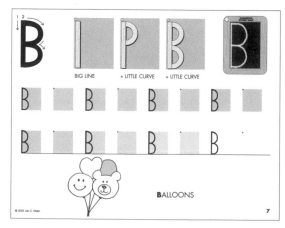

Teaching B

- Put your pencil on the dot (starting corner)—big line down—frog jump to the starting corner—little curve to the middle—little curve to the bottom corner.
- Don't lift the pencil when making the two little curves.
- Help children make the two little curves close to the same size.
- Tomorrow, review B before introducing R.

Teaching R

- Put your pencil on the dot (starting corner)—big line down—frog jump to the starting corner—little curve to the middle—little line slides down.
- Don't lift the pencil after making the little curve. Just stop and slide.
- Tomorrow, review R before introducing N.

Teaching N

- Put your pencil on the dot (starting corner)—big line down—frog jump to the starting corner—big line slides to the bottom corner—big line up like a helicopter.
- After the frog jump, N is made with a continuous stroke—don't lift the pencil off the page.
- Tomorrow, review N before introducing M.

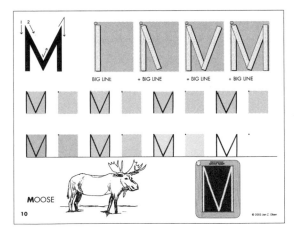

Teaching M

- Put your pencil on the dot (starting corner)—big line down—frog jump to the starting corner—big line slides to the middle bottom—climb up to corner—big line down.
- After the frog jump, M is made with a continuous stroke—don't lift the pencil off the page.
- Tomorrow, review M before starting the Mystery Letter Game.

Mystery Letter Game
Frog Jump Capitals — F E D P B R N M

Key Point: With this game children develop the correct habits for forming these capital letters.

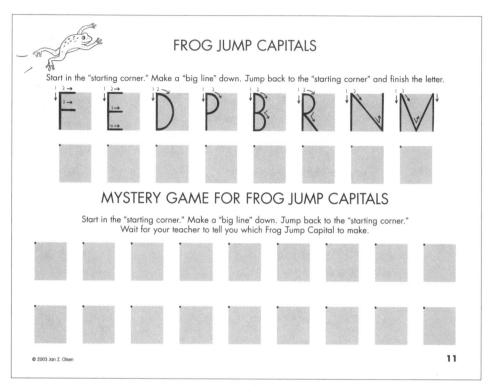

Lesson Plan

Demonstrate

Show children how to copy the Frog Jump Capitals and then play the Mystery Letter Game on the gray blocks.

Teach in workbook

At the top of the page:
1. Find the review letters.
2. Copy below each model. Follow the number and arrow directions with each letter for the proper formation sequence.

Play the Mystery Letter Game:
1. Put pencil on the dot (starting corner).
2. Make a big line down.
3. Frog Jump back to the starting corner.
4. Now make the mystery letter. The mystery letter is D (or F, E, M, N, R, P, or B, in random order). Remember the name of the letter is a secret. Do not name the mystery letter until children have made the big line down and jumped back to the starting corner.

With this game children will always use correct habits. They will start at the top and there will be no reversals. When the starting line is on the left edge, the next part of the letter will always be on the right side.

Tip

• Be sure all letters begin correctly. Children are happy to check one another to be sure everyone starts on the dot.

40

Mystery Letter Game
Frog Jump Capitals — F E D P B R N M

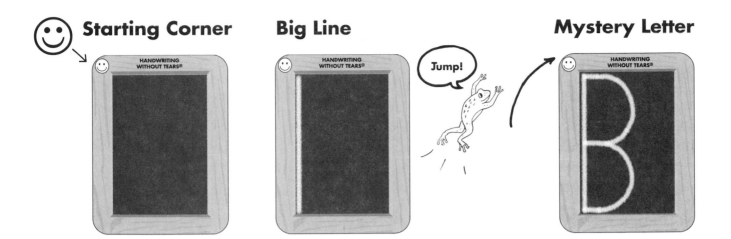

Starting Corner **Big Line** **Mystery Letter**

Jump!

Lesson Plan

Play the Mystery Letter Game on HWT Slates

Teachers will want to play this game on the HWT slates. This game is so much fun for your class when it's done on the slate.

Students put slates flat on their desk with the smiley face at the top. (Ask children to check their neighbors.) Have children show you their chalk by lifting hands in the air. Then say:

1. Put the chalk in the starting corner (by the smiley face).
2. Make a big line down.
3. Frog Jump back to the starting corner. Ribbit!
4. Now make the mystery letter. The mystery letter is B (or F, E, D, P, R, N or M, in random order). You may want to have the children hold the slates up for you to see and compliment.

What Are We Learning?

- To start at the top.
- To make letters in the correct sequence of strokes, from top to bottom, left to right.
- To place letters correctly so there are no reversals.

Tips

- Because children don't know which letter you will name, they never use old bad habits for letters. They simply start the mystery letter correctly and then make every letter correctly.
- A plain tissue makes a satisfactory eraser. You may also ask children to bring a small sock from home to use as an eraser and to hold chalk.
- Small pieces of chalk help your students develop the correct pinch for holding the pencil.

Teaching the
STARTING CORNER CAPITALS

Key Points: The Starting Corner Capitals, H K L U V W X Y Z, start in the starting corner. The first group, H K L, begins with a big line. Use the lesson plan for H as a general guide for all Starting Corner Capitals.

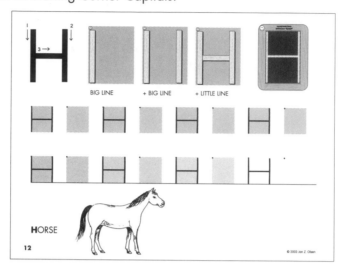

BIG LINE   + BIG LINE   + LITTLE LINE

HORSE

12   © 2003 Jan Z. Olsen

Lesson Plan

Demonstrate H

Show children how to make H on the HWT Slate Chalkboard or in the workbook. Say the step-by-step directions as you demonstrate. "Start in the starting corner— big line down—jump to the other top corner—big line down—jump to the middle of the first big line—little line across."

Teach in workbook

1. At the top of the page:
  - Find and finger trace the big, bold H. Follow the arrows, saying the step-by-step directions.
  - Review the pictures of making H with the HWT Wood Pieces Set.
  - Find and finger trace the H on the picture of the slate.

2. In the gray blocks:
  - Find H in the gray block.
  - Copy H. Put your pencil on the dot (starting corner)—big line down—jump to the other top corner—big line down—jump to the first big line in the middle—little line across.
  - Complete the first row of gray blocks. Save the second row for tomorrow.

3. At the bottom of the page:
  - Look at the word HORSE and the picture.
  - Find H in HORSE. Say HORSE. Make the H sound.
  - Color the horse. Extra: Name words that start with H. Draw a HAT or a HOUSE.

Tips

  - Introduce one new capital letter each day.
  - For H, left-handed children may make the little line from right to left.
  - Tomorrow, review H before introducing K.

Evaluate

  - If there are problems finding the middle for the little line across:
    Don't worry if it is a little high or low, just make sure it goes from one big line all the way to the other and that the children use the correct sequence of strokes.

42

© 2003 Jan Z. Olsen

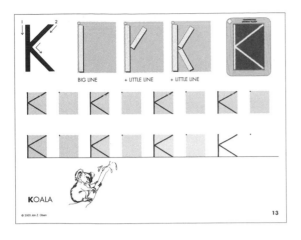

Teaching K

- Put your pencil on the dot (starting corner)—big line down—jump to the other corner—slide a little line to the middle of the big line—slide a little line down to the other bottom corner.
- Use the Karate K story to teach K: The karate teachers are going to demonstrate. This is Mr. Kaye, a karate teacher. (Put pencil in starting corner. Make a big line down.) This is Mrs. Kelly. She is a karate teacher too. (Put pencil in the other top corner.) Mrs. Kelly kicks Mr. Kaye right in the middle. Hi . . .Yaaa! (Make a karate kick with the pencil.)
- The kick part of the K is made with a continuous stroke. Don't lift the pencil off the page.
- Tomorrow, review K before introducing L.

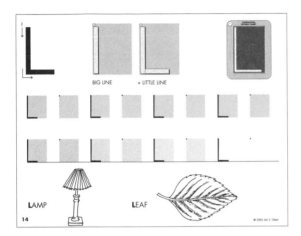

Teaching L

- Put your pencil on the dot (starting corner)—big line down—little line across.
- We suggest that left-handed children make the little line of L from left to right. Encouraging a continuous stroke will help! Don't pick up the pencil at the end of the big line down.
- It doesn't matter if the little line goes all the way across or not.
- Tomorrow, review L before introducing U.

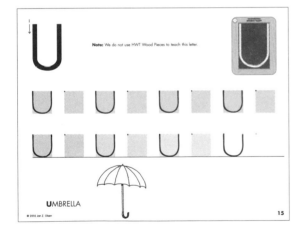

Teaching U

- U is taught on the slate using the Wet–Dry–Try technique. Do not teach U using the wood pieces.
- Put your pencil on the dot (starting corner)—big line down—curve all the way across bottom—big line up to the other corner.
- U uses a continuous stroke.

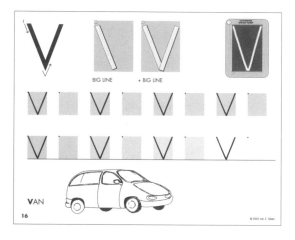

Teaching V

- Put your pencil on the dot (starting corner)—big line slides down and up.
- V uses a continuous stroke. Do not lift the pencil.
- Tomorrow, review V before introducing W.

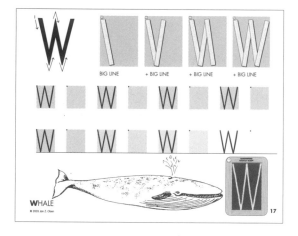

Teaching W

- Put your pencil on the dot (starting corner)—big line slides down and up, down and up.
- W is made with a continuous stroke. Do not lift the pencil.
- Tomorrow, review W before introducing X.

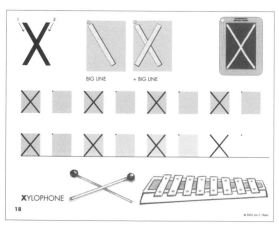

Teaching X

- Put your pencil on the dot (starting corner)—big line slides down to the bottom corner—jump to the other top corner—big line slides down the other way to the other bottom corner.
- Tomorrow, review X before introducing Y.

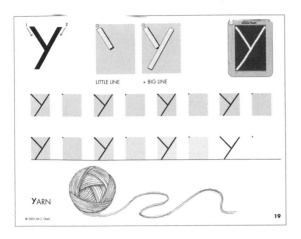

Teaching Y

- Put your pencil on the dot (starting corner)—little line slides down to the middle of the gray block—jump to the other top corner—big line slides to meet the little line and continues to the bottom corner.
- The length of the first line determines where the child's big line will hit the bottom. Do not worry too much about where it hits the bottom.
- Tomorrow, review Y before introducing Z.

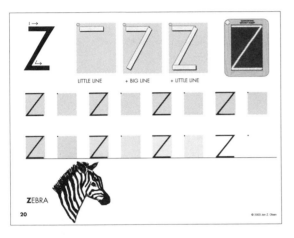

Teaching Z

- Put your pencil on the dot (starting corner)—little line across the top—big line slides down to the bottom corner—little line across.
- Tomorrow, review Z before starting the Words for Me review.

Teaching Words for Me

Many safety and information signs use capital letters. Explain that people use capitals for important signs. Depending on your students' needs, take one or two days to complete the page. Teachers should demonstrate, watch, and coach students.

- Look at the picture or symbol.
- Find the words in the gray blocks.
- Say the words and describe where children have seen the signs.
- Copy the words on the gray blocks below.

Teaching the
CENTER STARTERS

Key Points: The Center Starter Capitals, C O Q G S A I T J, start at the top center. The first group, C O Q G, begins with a "Magic C." Use the lesson plan for C as a general guide for all the Center Starters.

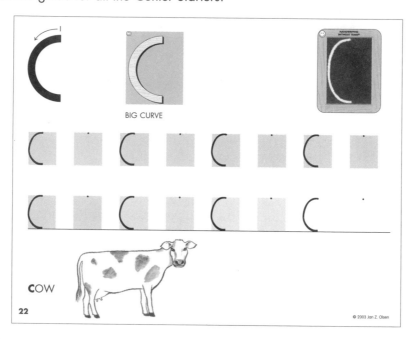

BIG CURVE

COW

22   © 2003 Jan Z. Olsen

Lesson Plan

Demonstrate C

Show children how to make C on the HWT Slate Chalkboard or in the workbook. Say the step-by-step directions as you demonstrate. "Start at the top center—big curve to the bottom."

Teach in workbook

1. At the top of the page:
- Find and finger trace the big bold C. Follow the arrow, saying the step-by-step directions.
- Review the picture of making C with a big curve.
- Find and finger trace the C on the picture of the slate.

2. In the gray blocks:
- Find C in the gray block.
- Copy C. "Put your pencil on the dot (top center)—big curve."
- Complete the first row of gray blocks. Save the second row for tomorrow.

3. At the bottom of the page:
- Look at the word COW and the picture.
- Find C in COW. Say COW. Make the C sound.
- Color the cow. Extra: Name words that start with C. Draw a CAR or a CAT.

Tips
- Spend extra time on C because the children are learning a new skill—starting at the top center—and because C is the basis for forming capitals O Q and G.
- C starts in the center and then goes toward the smiley face. Tell children to say "Hello" to the smiley face, but don't stay!
- Introduce one new capital letter each day.
- Tomorrow, review C before introducing O.

46

© 2003 Jan Z. Olsen

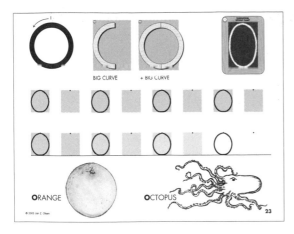

Teaching O

- Put your pencil on the dot (top center)—make a "Magic C"—keep on going—stop at the top center.
- Make sure students start O with a C stroke. Even left-handed students should make O this way. If students make O incorrectly, play the Mystery Letter Game described at the bottom of this page.
- Tomorrow, review O before introducing Q.

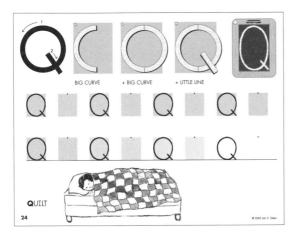

Teaching Q

- Put your pencil on the dot (top center)—make a "Magic C"—keep on going—stop at the top center—jump down and make a little line.
- Make sure students start Q with a C stroke. If they do it the other way, use the Mystery Letter Game below to correct this.
- Tomorrow, review Q before introducing G.

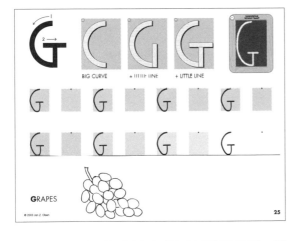

Teaching G

- Put your pencil on the dot (top center)—make a "Magic C"—make a little line up—cross.
- For left-handed children, it is fine for them to cross the G from right to left, pulling into the hand.
- Tomorrow, review G before playing the Mystery Letter Game.

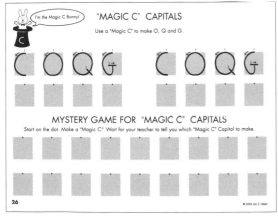

Teaching the Mystery Letter Game with "Magic C" Capitals, C O Q G

At the top of the page:
1. Find the review letters.
2. Copy below each model. Follow the step-by-step directions.

Play the Mystery Letter Game:
1. Put pencil on the dot (top center).
2. Make a "Magic C."
3. Now let's make the mystery letter. The mystery letter is G (or O or Q). With this game, children learn to start letters O Q G at the top with a "Magic C."

Teaching S

- Put your pencil on the dot (top center)—make a little curve (like a little "Magic C")—make a little curve going the other way.
- If children get stuck after the first little curve, tell them to "Stop, drop, and roll." Or try the slate Wet–Dry–Try activity.
- Tomorrow, review S before introducing A.

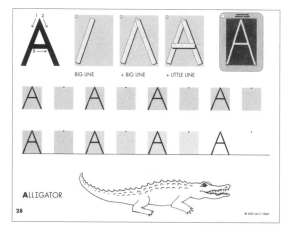

Teaching A

- Put your pencil on the dot (top center)—big line slides down to the corner—jump back to the dot (top center)—big line slides down to the other corner—little line across.
- Left-handed children may pull the little line across from right to left.
- Tomorrow, review A before introducing I.

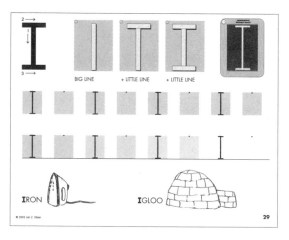

Teaching I

- Put your pencil on the dot (top center)—big line straight down to bottom—little line across top—little line across bottom.
- Left-handed children may make the little lines from right to left, pulling into the hand.
- Tomorrow, review I before introducing T.

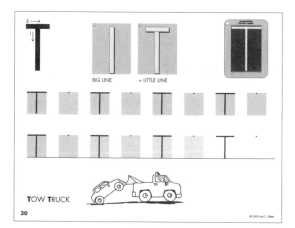

Teaching T

- Put your pencil on the dot (top center)—big line straight down to bottom—little line across the top.
- Left-handed children may make the little line from right to left, pulling into the hand.
- Show children how to make a T with their hands for time-out.
- Tomorrow, review T before introducing J.

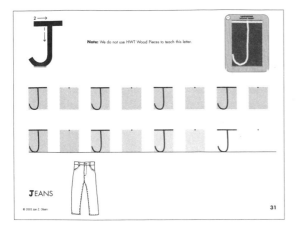

Teaching J

- Put your pencil on the dot (top center)—big line down—near the bottom make a J turn—little line across the top.
- Spend extra time tracing the J on the slate and explain that J turns toward the smiley face side.
- J is taught on the slate using the Wet–Dry–Try activity. Do not teach J using the wood pieces.
- Left-handed children may make the little line from right to left, pulling into the hand.
- Tomorrow, review J before starting the Words for Me review.

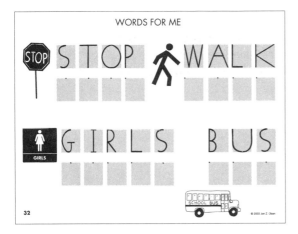

Teaching Words for Me

Many safety and information signs use capital letters. Explain that people use capitals for important signs. Depending on your students' needs, take one or two days to complete the page. Teachers should demonstrate, watch, and coach students.

- Look at the picture or symbol.
- Find the words in the gray blocks.
- Say the words and describe where they have seen the signs.
- Copy the words on the gray blocks below.

Extra:

Make a collection of road, safety, and information signs that use capitals. Have the children copy those words.

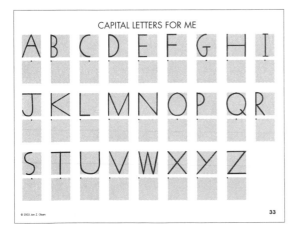

Teaching Capital Letters for Me

Copy this page! Use the ABCs for regular review. Even when your students are learning lowercase printing, they still need to keep up their capitals. Watch them write and give help as needed. Send this page home or use it in the classroom. Here are some fun ways to use the page:

- Find and copy just the "Center Starters." A C G I J O Q S T
- Find and copy just the "Starting Corner- Starting Line" letters.
  You'll find them on just the first two rows. B D E F H K L M N P R
- Copy just one row, the beginning, middle or end of the alphabet. A B C D E F G H I – J K L M N O P Q R – S T U V W X Y Z Now open a dictionary at the beginning, middle or end! See what letters are there.

Numbers Made Easy

Children love numbers. From the time they first hold their fingers up to show how old they are, numbers are an important part of life. Learning to write numbers is easy. Teach them at any time. We do not use the wood pieces to teach numbers, but we often use the wood piece words—big line, little line, big curve, little curve. Numbers are taught first on slates and then on gray blocks. The slate and gray blocks help children orient themselves to placing numbers correctly.

Your children will learn to:
- Start numbers at the top.
- Use the correct stroke sequence to form the numbers.
- Place all numbers correctly without reversals.

Number Style

The numbers are simplified so that they all start exactly at the top and use very basic lines and curves.

1 2 3 4 5 6 7 8 9 10

Teaching Order

The numbers are taught and reviewed in numerical order.

Workbook Design

Letters and Numbers for Me gives each number its own page. Each page is clean and clear but filled with great learning opportunities. The new number is shown on a slate and the teacher gives directions. There is a big number to finger trace, animals or objects to count and color, and words to read (for example, one whale, two alligators). This means continual review. At the end of the number section is a complete review page to copy for additional practice.

Unique Teaching Strategies

Learning numbers is fun and reversal proof with the HWT slate chalkboard and the special gray blocks. Try teaching new numbers with the Wet–Dry–Try method (page 28 of this guide). This strategy is also described right in the workbook, *Letters and Numbers for Me,* on page 34. There are no reversals with this method.

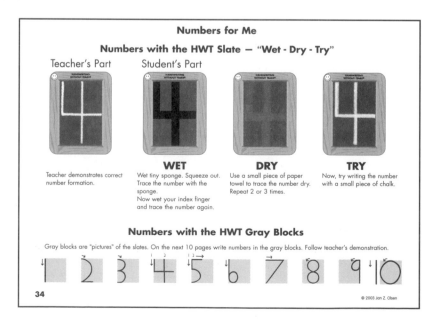

50

Basic Lesson Plan: Use the plan below as a general guide for all numbers. Special tips for other numbers follow.

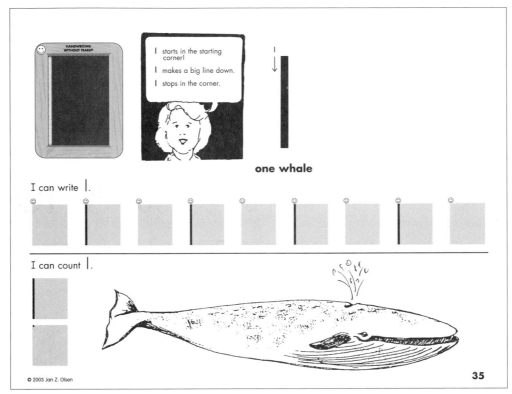

Numbers should be taught separately from handwriting, before a math-related activity. HWT teaches numbers with the Wet–Dry–Try method on the slate and gray blocks.

Lesson Plan

Demonstrate 1

Show children how to make 1 on the slate and/or in the workbook. Say the step-by-step directions as you demonstrate.

Teach in workbook

1. Explain that the gray block is a little picture of the slate.
2. Find the starting corner ☺.
3. Copy the 1. Teacher should demonstrate, coach, and watch students.
   Note: Tell left-handed students to copy from the model on the right.

Tips

- Reading: Have students find and read the words "one whale." Talk about the word one and the symbol 1. Students may also read "I can write 1" and "I can count 1."
- Coloring: Students may color the whale and add water and other sea animals. This is for children who finish first and like to color.

Evaluate

- Finger tracing the large number is a quick way to check the students' top-to-bottom habit before letting them practice.

TEACHING 2

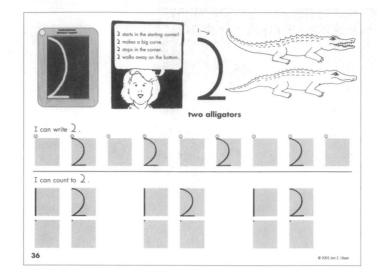

two alligators

Wait until 1 is secure before teaching 2.
Can the child write 1 correctly from memory?
Use the basic lesson plan and these tips for 2.

 Tips for 2

2 wants to start in the starting corner.

- Don't be anxious if 2 is a little fat, or a little skinny. As children gain skill, the 2 will develop a nice shape.
- Exaggerate pushing the chalk into the bottom corner of the slate (same with the pencil on the gray block). This promotes a nice sharp point.
- The little line ends just under the curve of the 2. Don't worry if it goes all the way across. This is not an important issue.

TEACHING 3

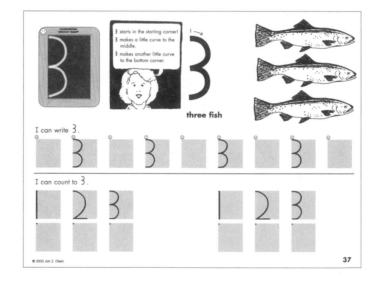

three fish

Wait until 2 is secure before teaching 3.
Can the child write 2 correctly from memory?
Use the basic lesson plan and these tips for 3.

 Tips for 3

3 wants to start in the starting corner too!

- Some children have trouble finding the middle. Use a body image of a head (smiley face), tummy (middle), and feet (bottom of slate) to help them. It works for the gray block too.
- Make the chalk bump the wood at the middle. This promotes a nice sharp point.
- Don't worry if the little curves are fat, skinny, or not exactly equal. They'll improve.

52

TEACHING 4

Wait until 3 is secure before teaching 4.
Can the child write 3 correctly from memory?
Use the basic lesson plan and these tips for 4.

☺ Tips for 4

4 wants to start in the starting corner too!

- Some children need help stopping at the middle. Ask the child to point to the middle before starting the little line down.
- Make sure the horizontal little line goes all the way across the slate or gray block.
- Add sound effects (ooo's) when 4 "walks across the dark night!"

TEACHING 5

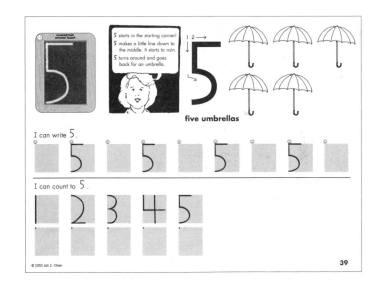

Wait until 4 is secure before teaching 5.
Can the child write 4 correctly from memory?
Use the basic lesson plan and these tips for 5.

☺ Tips for 5

5 wants to start in the starting corner too!

- Don't let children make 5 in a continuous stroke. That style deteriorates into an S shape with use.
- The two-step 5 stays neat in use.
- Expand the story by saying 5 is a bald man who walks down the street. He feels rain on his head, and turns around to go back for his umbrella. Tell them to look at the smiley face—that's the bald man.

TEACHING 6

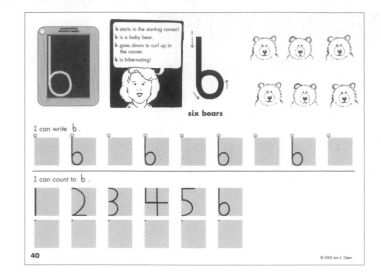

six bears

I can write 6.

I can count to 6.

1 2 3 4 5 6

40

© 2003 Jan Z. Olsen

Wait until 5 is secure before teaching 6. Can the child write 5 correctly from memory?
Use the basic lesson plan and these tips for 6.

 Tips for 6

6 wants to start in the starting corner too! (Some people think it should start in the center, but if it did, it could be reversed.)

- Don't worry if it looks straight for awhile. With a little use, it will curve naturally.
- Don't worry about kids thinking it's letter b. (They don't use numbers and letters together until Algebra!)
- If you live in a hot climate, you can skip the bears. For example, in Texas 6 could be an armadillo.

TEACHING 7

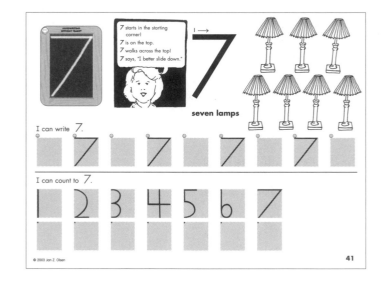

seven lamps

I can write 7.

I can count to 7.

1 2 3 4 5 6 7

© 2003 Jan Z. Olsen

41

Wait until 6 is secure before teaching 7.
Can the child write 6 correctly from memory?
Use the basic lesson plan and these tips for 7.

 Tips for 7

7 wants to start in the starting corner too!

- Act out this 7 story for your students. Put a smiley face in the top left corner of a door frame. Reach up and put your fingers on the smiley face. Say that when you're out of the room 7 "walks" across the top of the door. "Walk" your fingers across the top. 7 hears you coming and says, "Get down fast! Here she comes."
- If you have a student who cannot do diagonals, the 7 can go straight down.

54

TEACHING 8

Wait until 7 is secure before teaching 8.
Can the child write 7 correctly from memory?
Teach letter S before 8.
Use the basic lesson plan and these tips for 8.

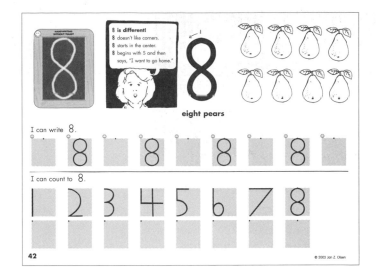

Tips for 8

8 starts in the center.

- 8 says, "I don't have any corners. I don't like corners. I won't start in a corner. I want to start in the center!"
- 8 (like I and O) is a symmetrical letter and can't be reversed.
- Starting 8 correctly can be a problem. Just pretend the 8 wants to go over to say "Hi" to the smiley face to start the first curve. Teach S before 8. If S has been learned, then 8 is easier.
- For both S and 8, children often stop after the first curve and don't know what to do. Tell them to "STOP, DROP, AND ROLL" (fire safety). This will get them going the right way. The repetitions of the Wet–Dry–Try activity are very useful for children who have trouble with 8.

TEACHING 9

Wait until 8 is secure before teaching 9.
Can the child write 8 correctly from memory?
Use the basic lesson plan and these tips for 9.

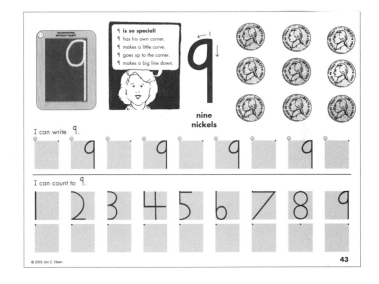

Tips for 9

9 starts in the other corner (top right).

- Children get a kick out of 9 complaining about how long he had to wait for his turn. I say that 9 insists on having his own private corner.
- Use the helicopter image and sound effects.

TEACHING 10

Wait until 9 is secure before teaching 10.
Can the child write 9 correctly from memory?
Use the lesson plan and these tips for 10.

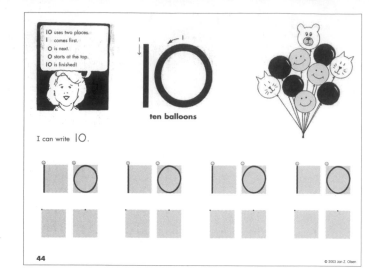

Tips for 10

10 is the first time two places are used.
- Children already know how to make 1. It starts in the starting corner with a big line down.
- The zero begins at the top with a C stroke just like letter O.

Numbers for Me

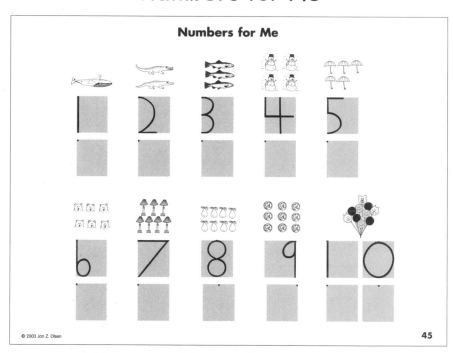

- Make copies of this page for extra practice.
- Student copies number below the model.

Special way to correct papers:

Use this friendly strategy to solve reversal problems.
1. Check arithmetic or "counting" papers.
2. Mark only one reversal per paper. Mark the lowest number. Ignore all others.
3. Show the child how to make the number correctly by using the slate or gray block.

Gradually all reversals will be eliminated. You will always teach the lowest number and it will get all the help it needs.
With this structure, your children will learn to write numbers correctly and automatically.

Lowercase Letters Made Easy

HWT Letter Style

HWT uses a simple, continuous-stroke, vertical style. The vertical style is very important for young children because vertical lines come first in normal child development. Diagonal letters are difficult for young children. We would never use a slanted italic because it is inappropriate developmentally. Vertical letters are easier for young children to read and write and they're like the ones children see in daily life. We use a continuous stroke for lowercase letters, so the children learn the letters the same way they'll write them in first grade.

a b c d e f g h i j k l m n o p q r s t u v w x y z

Teaching Order

Individually, you may teach a few letters out of order. Do this for the letters in children's names. Children need and want to write their names correctly. The teaching order in the book is based on:

- Complexity of the letter—Letters that are easy to form or like the capital are taught earlier.
- Formation patterns—Letters that use the same strokes are generally grouped together.
- Frequency of use—This was determined by counting letters in the Dolch word lists for Grades K , 1, and 2. The frequency of letter use order is:

    e o a t n s h i l r w u d y m f k g b p c v j q z x

- Possibility of reversal—Letters that children may confuse (b and d and g, q, and p) are separated by many pages.

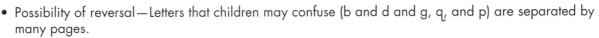

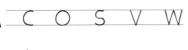
We start with c o s v w because they are easy—they are the same as their capital partners, just smaller. They all start on the top line and fit between the HWT double lines.

Lowercase t is like capital T, but is crossed lower. This is the first letter children learn that starts above the double lines.

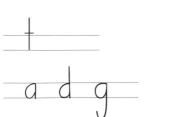
The "Magic c" letters, a d and g, all begin with a c stroke. They are also frequently used letters.

These letters complete the vowels. Letter e is difficult to write but is the most frequently used letter.

This is a transition group. Letters l and k begin above the HWT double lines, and y and j descend below.

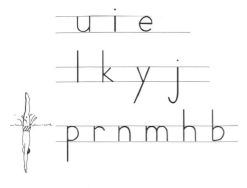
The diver letters, p r n m h and b, use a similar stroke pattern: "dive down, come up, and swim over to the right." We avoid b and d confusion by separating these letters by many pages. Further, by teaching b after h, children will write b using the correct stroke order.

This is the final group. Letter f is taught here because it has a difficult starting stroke. Letter q is taught here to avoid confusion with g. Letters x and z are capital partners but are introduced last because of their infrequent use.

Workbook Design

Huge Step-by-Step Illustrated Directions

To really understand correct letter formation, children need to see each step in sequence. Tiny direction arrows on a picture of a finished letter simply won't do! In *Letters and Numbers for Me,* each letter has a demonstration is big enough to be finger traced. Finger tracing helps children learn through their tactile (touch) and kinesthetic (movement) senses.

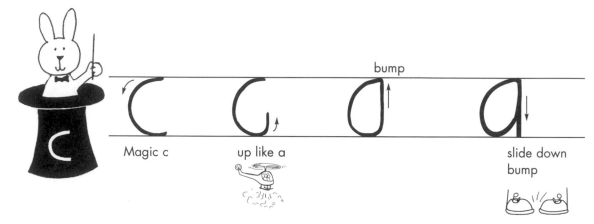

Magic c   up like a   bump   slide down bump

Child-Friendly, Consistent Terminology

Letters and Numbers for Me uses child-friendly words to describe each step for making the letters (see the example above). Young children will know what you mean when you say "Magic 'c,' up like a helicopter, bump, slide down, bump." There is no strange jargon or indecipherable terminology. The books are for children and use language and symbols that they understand. Read the directions out loud to the students. This helps your auditory (hearing) learners remember how to form the letters correctly.

HWT Double Lines

All of the HWT workbooks use double guidelines. The bottom line keeps the writing straight and the top line controls the size. The double lines end the problem of line confusion. Trying to follow typical beginner lined paper is like learning to drive on a four lane freeway—a blue line at the top, a dotted line in the middle, a red line on the bottom, and another blue line below. It is easy to understand why so many children have trouble.

Just two lines are easy.

On the HWT double lines 14 letters fit exactly between the double lines and most letters (19 out of 26!) begin exactly on the top line. The children find it easy to notice and place the letters that go above the lines and the letters that go below. They have more control, confidence, and size consistency using HWT double lines.

Sentences for Me

I like tacos.

Fair Practice

In the workbooks we never ask the child to copy or use a letter that has not been taught. The words and sentences that we give for practice use only the letters that the children already know.

Copy One Time Only from Each Model

Too much practice can make a child's writing worse. Have you seen papers or workbooks where they give a child a model of the letter or word along the left side of the page and then the child is supposed to copy it over and over across the page? The child copies the model and then copies the copy of the model, and so on. The letters get progressively worse. It's boring. It's much better to have the child make just one letter beside each model.

S s s s s

When practicing words, children write each word once beside the model.

keep   keep

Not Just Letters, But Words Too!

The focus of the book is on letters, but children need to use and review the letters they learn. The special pages, Words for Me, use the child's new letters in very simple words. This gives letter review while teaching beginning word skills.

Room to Write

Little children need extra room to write. They are just beginners and they don't print with precision. On the Words for Me pages, there is plenty of room for the child to copy the word. Only HWT workbooks give children enough room to write.

The generous spacing in the HWT workbooks teaches good word and sentence spacing habits. The Sentences for Me page shows the extremely generous spaces recommended for kindergarten students. This prevents children from runningtheirwordstogether. Huge spaces between words make it easy for young children to read and copy word by word.

Words for Me

COW   COW

WOW   WOW

Left-Hand Friendly Design

Letters and Numbers for Me, like all the HWT workbooks, is left-hand friendly. Each letter page is designed so that both right- and left-handed children have a model to look at when they copy. The left-handed child is shown how to copy from the model on the right. On the Words for Me pages the word is repeated so that left-handed children never have to lift the hand or place it in an awkward position to see the model.

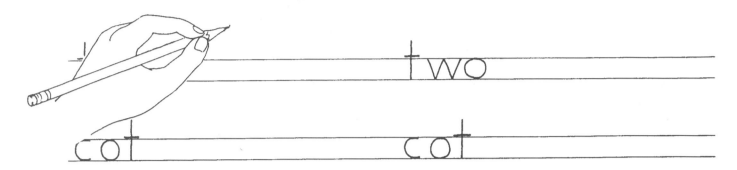

A G H I J T f t

Special exception: Left-handed people naturally make horizontal lines from right to left, pulling into the hand. Make sure you do not correct this as it is natural and not a problem. But for E, F, and L we suggest all children push off from the big line using a left-to-right stroke.

Simple Black-and-White Pages

This kindergarten workbook, like all HWT workbooks, has simple black-and-white pages that are clean and clear. We deliberately avoid the visual confusion of distracting background images, overdone colored graphics, multicolored lines, and crowded pages. These "fancy" effect can create visual perceptual difficulties for children and distract them.

The simple workbook pages keep children happy and occupied. In kindergarten some children finish writing their lessons before others. The children who finish first can color the pictures or add drawings to the pages. This is so nice because it makes the book more personal. It's also nice for the teacher as it keeps those children occupied.

Children enjoy seeing their own writing and coloring or drawing on the pages. They like that the models are handwritten. Their writing looks like the writing in the book. HWT workbooks celebrate the child's work.

Left-to-Right Directionality

This is an exciting, unique feature of the HWT workbooks. Look at the illustrations! They promote left-to-right directionality. The alligator, cow, tow truck, and other drawings are going from left to right across the page to encourage correct visual tracking and writing from left to right on the page. Young children are learning that people read and write English from left to right.

60

Unique Teaching Strategies

Magic c, up like a helicopter, bump, slide down, bump

Demonstrate with Voices at the Blackboard

Key Point: This is so much fun that children will watch and pay attention for seven demonstrations of the same letter!

Prepare
1. Premark the double lines on the chalkboard.
2. Begin at the far left of the board.
3. Have the students open their workbooks, find the step-by-step directions, and read the words out loud with them.

Demonstrate
1. Demonstrate the letter, describing each step.
2. Say the words that are in the workbook.
3. Ask the children to say the words with you.

Demonstrate Again and Again, But Never Bore Them!
1. Demonstrate the letter and say the words with **high** voices.
2. Demonstrate the letter and say the words with **low** voices.
3. Demonstrate the letter and say the words with **loud** voices.
4. Demonstrate the letter and say the words with **soft** voices.
5. Demonstrate the letter and say the words with **slow** voices.
6. Demonstrate the letter and say the words with **fast** voices.

Results
1. Your children will know how to make each part of the letter.
2. They will memorize the words for each step.
3. They will be able to talk themselves through making the letter.

Tips
- If using a blackboard, wet the board and write the double lines. They'll stay until you remove them with a damp cloth.
- If using a whiteboard, mark the double lines with a "wet erase" pen. Then write the letters with a "dry erase" pen. Your lines will stay on the board when you erase. Use a damp cloth to erase the double lines.

Multisensory Learning with Wet-Dry-Try

What children do, they remember. Bring your children to the board after you've demonstrated a letter several times. They have seen and heard your demonstration and they've said the words. Now they'll trace over the letter with a little wet sponge. They'll feel how to make the letter as they make the correct arm and hand movements. Here's how to do this: Prepare a dish of small damp sponges. Have a small group (one child for each letter you've made) come to the board to "wet" the letters. The next group can "dry" the letter with a small piece of paper towel. The last group can "try" with chalk.

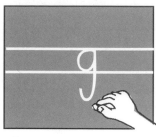

Demonstrate

The teacher teaches the letter by demonstration and describing each step.

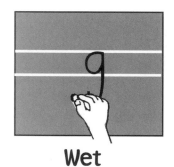

Wet

Wet the teacher's chalk letter by tracing over it with a tiny wet sponge.

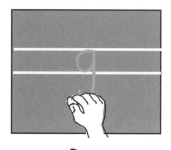

Dry

Dry the letter with a piece of paper towel.

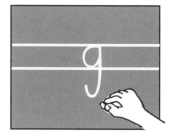

Try

Try writing the letter with chalk.

Demonstrate at the Whiteboard

If you have whiteboards you will demonstrate there. While you won't be able to use the Wet–Dry–Try technique, you can have children erase with a tissue to give them the opportunity to write large on a vertical surface.

Demonstrate in the Workbooks

Children need to see you write in their workbooks. Demonstrate the letter once for them and then have them make one for you. After you watch, you'll know if they need help and where help is needed. A few children need to watch more than once. Demonstrate the letter two times. Then ask, "Do you want to see it again before you try?" Children are so savvy about knowing how many times they need to see it. Let them tell you.

Pleasing Practice

Children love the short practice! The focus is always on using correct habits and doing one's best work, not on finishing a page! Lessons are about 10 minutes a day with just 5 minutes of actual practice time. The focus of our practice is on the process, not the product. With correct practice, the product will naturally improve. The teacher must be sure that the child is practicing the correct habits.

Teaching Lowercase Letters
Teaching c o s v w

TEACHING ORDER

C O S V W
t
a d g
u i e l k y j
p r n m h b
f q x z

Key Points: Children know these letters from capitals. They learn that lowercase c o s v w are the same as C O S V W, just lower. They learn to place the lowercase letters on the double lines. Use the lesson plan for c as a general guide for o s v and w.

Letters and Numbers for Me
page 47

Magic c

c is for **c**ow.

47

Lesson Plan

Demonstrate c
Show children how to make c on the board and/or in the workbook.
Start at the top. Make a c stroke. Say the words "Magic c."

Teach in workbook
1. Find the picture of the Magic c Bunny.
   Read "Magic c."
   Finger trace the huge c.
2. Find C on the gray block and c on the double lines.
   Copy the c's. Teacher should demonstrate, coach, and watch students.
3. Read "C is for cow." Move finger under the sentence from left to right.
   Find C and c in the sentence. Color the cow and draw grass for the cow.

CAPITAL   lowercase

Tips
- Teach that the C and c are the same, but lowercase c is lower.
- Show the difference between C and c: hold up your left hand flat and say, "This is Capital C." Hold right hand up fisted. Say, "This is lowercase c. It's lower!"
- Teach students to start exactly on the dot.
- Emphasize "bumping" or touching the bottom line.
- Tell left-handed students to look at the model on the right.

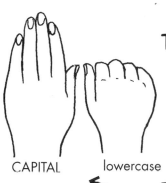

HANDWRITING WITHOUT TEARS®

Evaluate
- If c is too skinny:
  Start on the dot and then travel ⟵ on the top line before curving down.
  This will make for a bigger curve.
- If c is reversed:
  Teach C on the slate. Start in the top center and move chalk toward the ☺ side.
  Use the Wet–Dry–Try method if needed.

Teaching O

- Teach that O and o are the same, but lowercase o is lower.
- Teach students to start exactly on the dot.
- Emphasize bumping the bottom line.
- If o doesn't start at the top, or goes the wrong way:
  Use the slate. Start in the top center and move chalk toward the ☺ side in a c stroke.
  Use the Wet–Dry–Try method if needed.

Teaching S

- Teach that S and s are the same, but lowercase s is lower.
- Teach students to start exactly on the dot.
- Emphasize bumping the bottom line.
- If letter s doesn't start at the top, or goes the wrong way:
  Use the slate. Start at the top center and move chalk toward the ☺ side with a little c stroke.
- If child has problem changing directions for s:
  Use the Wet–Dry–Try method.

Teaching V

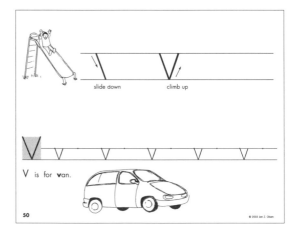

- Teach that V and v are the same, but lowercase v is lower.
- Teach students to start exactly on the dot.
- Emphasize bumping the bottom line and then the top line.
- If child has problems with diagonal lines:
  Teach V on the slate. V starts in the starting corner.
  Use the slate Wet–Dry–Try method.
  Use real-life experiences with slides and ramps.
- Have child make a v with index and middle finger.

Teaching W

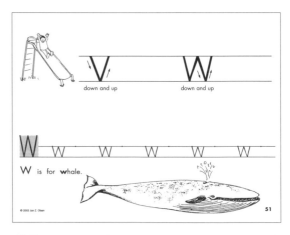

- Teach that W and w are the same, but lowercase w is lower.
- Teach students to start exactly on the dot.
- Emphasize bumping the bottom line and then the top line, bottom and top.
- If child has problems with diagonal lines:
  Go back and work on v.

64

Teaching †

Key Points: Lowercase t is the first letter that starts above the double lines. Lowercase t is the same as capital T except that lowercase t is crossed lower.

Letters and Numbers for Me
page 52

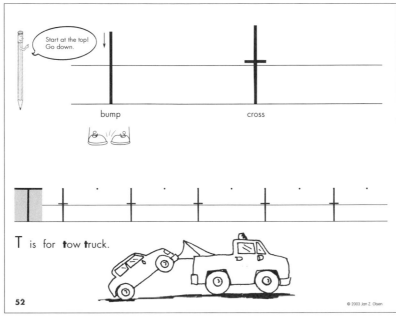

Start at the top! Go down.

bump   cross

T is for tow truck.

52

© 2003 Jan Z. Olsen

TEACHING ORDER

c o s v w
†
a d g
u i e l k y j
p r n m h b
f q x z

Lesson Plan

Demonstrate †

Show the difference between T and t by having children make T and t with their hands.
Show children how to make t on the board and/or in the workbook.
Say the step-by-step directions as you demonstrate.

Teach in workbook

1. Read the directions.
   Finger trace the step-by-step models.
2. Find T on the gray block and t on the double lines.
   Copy the t's. Teacher should demonstrate, coach, and watch students.
   Note: Tell left-handed students to copy from the model on the right.
3. Read "T is for tow truck." Move finger under the sentence from left to right.
   Find T and t in the sentence. Color the tow truck.

Tips

- Teach that t is a tall lowercase letter. It starts above the lines.
- Teach students to start exactly on the dot.
- Children cross t according to their handedness.
  Right handed children cross from left to right.
  Teacher marks ⟶ for right handed students.
  Left-handed children cross from right to left, pulling into the hand.
  Teacher marks ⟵ for left handed students.

Evaluate

- If t starts on the bottom line:
  Have them point in the air and say, "T is for top. T starts at the top."

Teaching Words for Me

Key Points: The list of words on the left has a twin list in the middle of the page. Children learn to put letters close together when they write words. Children learn to leave space between the word model in the book and the word they write. This provides meaningful practice of the letters they have just learned.

Letters and Numbers for Me
page 53

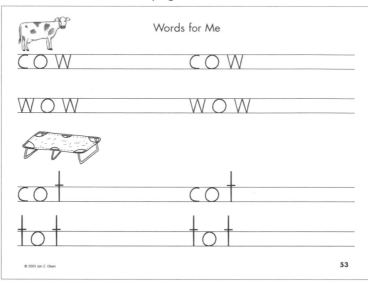

Lesson Plan
Demonstrate each word on the board using double lines
- Show children that letters in words are close together. Have them put their index fingers close together but not touching and say, "The letters are close but they don't touch."
- Show children how to print each word on the board and/or in the workbook.
- Describe each letter as you write.

Teach in workbook
1. Find the twin words. "Are they the same or different?" The same!
2. Read the words.
3. Leave a generous space before beginning to copy words.
4. Copy words from left to right. Left-handed students look at the middle column when they copy.

Tips
- Students copy each word one time. (Help left-handed students to look at the middle list.)
- Teach just two to four words a day. Copy from the first column one day and the second column the next.
- To show that letters in a word are close, have children put fingers very close, but not touching.

Evaluate
- If some letters aren't placed correctly on the lines:
  Teach that c o s v w are the same height and fit between the lines. Letter t should stick out because it starts higher.
- If letters are not placed close together in the word:
  Coach students to start the next letter by placing the pencil near the previous letter.
- If students run their words together:
  Say that you will give them what they need for spaces. Have them hold out their hands to catch it. Take a huge empty plastic bottle, or any container, and make a big show of pouring into their hands. Ask, "What did you get?" Nothing! Tell them to put nothing after every word they write.

Meet the Magic c Bunny!

Key Points: Key Points: The Magic c Bunny helps you teach the c-based lowercase letters o, a, d and g. The Magic c Bunny puppet will bring your lessons to life.

I'm the Magic c Bunny!

- The Magic c Bunny changes letter c into new letters. That's the magic trick!

- You may purchase a puppet from HWT. See page 1 for a photo of the puppet.

- You may follow the directions below to make a Magic c Bunny from a napkin.

Make a Magic c Bunny!

1
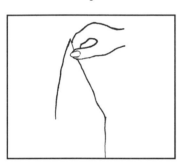
Open paper napkin. Hold by one corner.

2
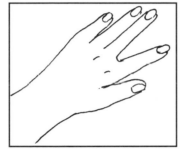
Spread index and middle fingers apart.

3
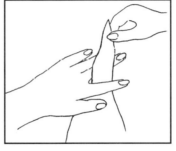
Pull corner between your index and middle fingers. (First ear)

4
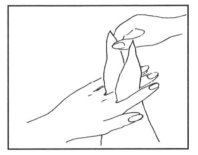
Take the next corner. Pull corner between your middle and ring fingers. (Second ear)

5
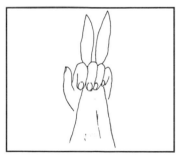
Fold fingers into palm.

6
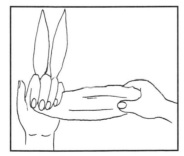
Pull napkin out to side.

7

Wrap napkin over fingers and tuck into hand.

8
Add the face with a pen. It's a bunny! You may slip the bunny off your fingers and give it to a child. Tape or staple the napkin to hold it.

Teaching the "Magic c" Letters
a d g

TEACHING ORDER

C o s v w
t
a d g
u i e l k y j
p r n m h b
f q x z

Key Points: Letters a d g do not look like capital A D G. Lowercase a d g are "Magic c" letters because they begin with a c stroke. They start on the top line and are made with a continuous stroke. Use the lesson plan for a as a general guide for d and g.

Letters and Numbers for Me
page 54

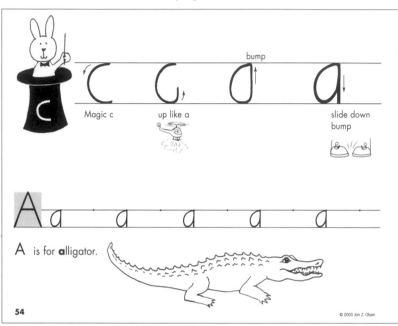

bump

Magic c   up like a   slide down bump

A a a a a a

A is for **a**lligator.

54   © 2003 Jan Z. Olsen

Lesson Plan

Demonstrate a
Show children how to make a on the board and/or in the workbook.
Say the step-by-step directions as you demonstrate.

Teach in workbook
1. Find the picture of the Magic c Bunny.
   Read the directions—"Magic c, up like a helicopter, up, slide down, bump."
   Finger trace the step-by-step model.
2. Find A on the gray block and a on the double lines.
   Copy the a's. Teacher should demonstrate, coach, and watch students.
   Note: Tell left-handed students to copy from the model on the right.
3. Read "A is for alligator." Move finger under the sentence from left to right.
   Find A and a in the sentence. Children may color the alligator.

Tip
• Teach that A D G and a d g are different.

Evaluate
• If a is too skinny:
  Start on the dot and travel on the top line before curving down.
• If child has a bad habit for making a:
  After teaching d and g, you will use the Mystery Letter Game for "Magic c" letters to correct this habit. See it on page 74 of this guide.

68   © 2003 Jan Z. Olsen

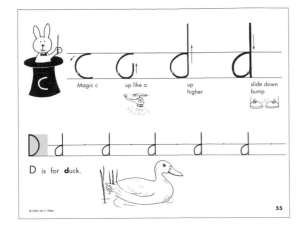

Teaching d

- Teach that D and d are different.
- Teach that d starts with a "Magic c."
- Teach that d goes above the double lines, but does not start above the lines.
- If child doesn't retrace line down:
  Tell child to think of sliding down a pole.
  "Hang on until your feet touch the ground."
- If child makes a short d:
  Tell child to go up higher in the helicopter.

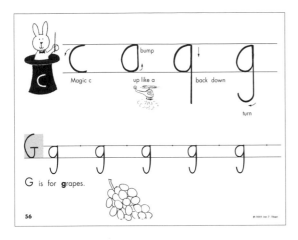

Teaching g

- Teach that G and g are different.
- Teach that g starts with a "Magic c."
- Teach that g goes down below the double lines.
- Teach the turn. Draw a little face in the g. That's George. He says, "Oooh, if I fall will you catch me?" Sure! Turn the g to catch George and it will always be turned correctly.

Mystery!!! Mastering "Magic c" Letters

Key Points: This game promotes correct habits and eliminates bad ones. Children will automatically begin letters a d g o correctly with a "Magic c" stroke.

Letters and Numbers for Me
page 57

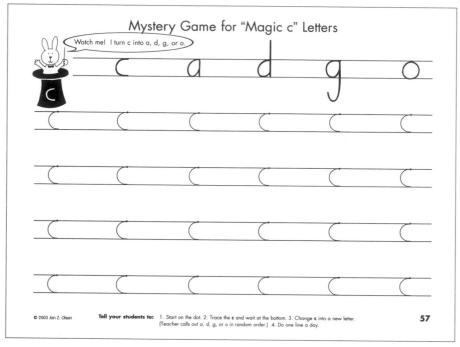

Lesson Plan

Demonstrate "Magic c" letters
Show children how each of the letters begins with c.
The letter c magically changes into a - d - g or o.

Teach in workbook
Wait for all students to put pencils on the dot. Tell students to:
1. Start on the dot.
2. Trace the c and wait at the bottom.
3. Now change c into a new letter (Call out a, d, g, or o in random order).

Tips
- Be careful not to name the letter first. The name of the letter is a secret! Because children don't know which letter they are making, they can't use bad habits.
- Complete just one line of letters a day. Spread this activity out over time for best results.
- Repeat the activity as needed until there are no problems with "Magic c" letters.

Evaluate
- Observe your children as they write the c-based letters. Do all begin with a "Magic c" stroke? Continue this game until correct habits are completely automatic. You can check with words like cow, cat, and dog.

70

Teaching Words for Me

Key Points: The list of words on the left has a twin list in the middle of the page. Children learn to put letters close together when they write words. Children learn to leave space between the word model in the book and the word they write. This provides meaningful practice of the letters they have just learned, a d g.

Letters and Numbers for Me
page 58

Lesson Plan

Demonstrate each word on the board using double lines

Show children that letters in words are close together. Have them put their index fingers close together, but not touching, and say, "The letters are close but they don't touch."
Show children how to print each word on the board and/or in the workbook.
Describe each letter as you write.

Teach in workbook

1. Find the twin words. "Are they the same or different?" The same!
2. Read the words.
3. Leave a generous space before beginning to copy words.
4. Copy words from left to right.

Tips

- Students copy each word one time.
- Teach just two to four words a day. Copy from the first column one day and the second column the next.
- Tell left-handed students to look at the middle list.

Evaluate

- If letters are not placed close together in the word:
  Coach students to start the next letter by placing the pencil near the previous letter.

Teaching u i e

TEACHING ORDER

c o s v w
t
a d g
u i e l k y j
p r n m h b
f q x z

Key Points: Letters u i e complete the vowels. They fit between the double lines. Use the lesson plan for u as a general guide for i and e.

Letters and Numbers for Me
page 59

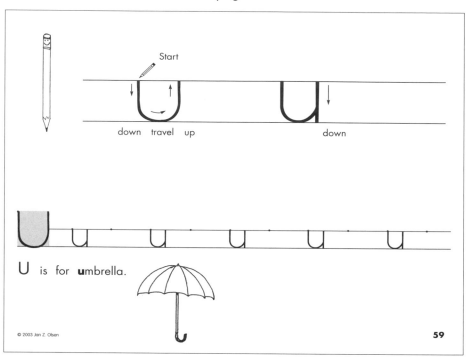

Start

down   travel   up   down

U is for **u**mbrella.

© 2003 Jan Z. Olsen   **59**

Lesson Plan

Demonstrate u

Show children how to make u on the board and/or in the workbook.
Say the step-by-step directions as you demonstrate.

Teach in workbook

1. Find the picture of the pencil.
   Read the directions—"Start, down, travel, up, down"
   Finger trace the step-by-step model.
2. Find U on the gray block and u on the double lines.
   Copy the u's. Teacher should demonstrate, coach, and watch students.
   Note: Tell left-handed students to copy from the model on the right.
3. Read "U is for umbrella." Move finger under the sentence from left to right. Find U and u in the sentence. Children may color the umbrella and add raindrops.

Tips

• U and u are almost the same. The only difference is the final line down on u.
• Teach careful retracing for line down.

Evaluate

• If u is too pointed like a v:
  Travel on the bottom line. Take at least "two steps" on the line and then come up straight.

72   © 2003 Jan Z. Olsen

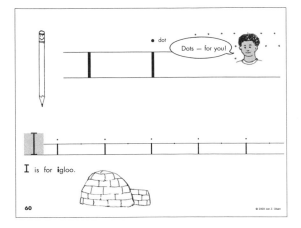

Teaching i

- Teach that I and i are different.
- Teach children to make the line down before adding the dot.
- If i is too short:
  Tell the child to place the pencil on the top line, then bump the bottom line.
- If the child makes a small circle to dot the i instead of a dot, it's okay. It's a personal style.

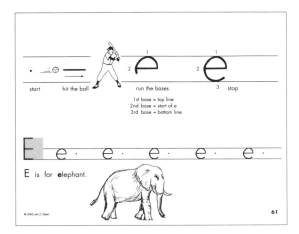

Teaching e

- Teach that E and e are different.
- Letter e is hard, but is the most frequently used letter.
- Lowercase e does not begin on a line—it begins in the air between the lines.
- Remind the child that it is not a home run, so only run to 3rd base.
- If beginning line isn't straight:
  Have student practice writing straight dashes between the lines.

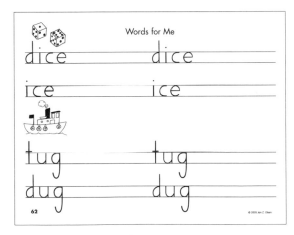

Teaching Words for Me

- Provides meaningful practice of the letters they have just learned,
  u i e.
- Students copy each word one time. (Help left-handed students to look at the middle list.)
- Teach just two to four words a day.

Teaching Sentences for Me

Key Points: Children learn to begin a sentence with a capital letter, leave space between words, and end with a period. Very generous spaces between words give young children room to write.

Letters and Numbers for Me
page 63

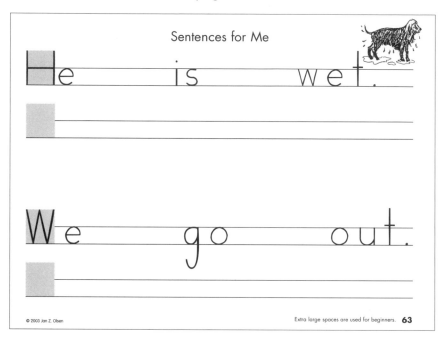

Lesson Plan

Teach in workbook

1. Begin sentences with a capital letter on the gray block.
2. Students copy directly under each word.
3. Leave space between words! The sentences use very generous spaces. Exaggerating the spaces now will result in beautiful sentence spacing as a habit.
4. End with a period.

Evaluate

- If students run their words together:
  Say that you will give them what they need for spaces. Have them hold out their hands to catch it. Take a huge empty plastic bottle or any container and make a big show of pouring into their hands. Ask, "What did you get?" Nothing! Tell them to put nothing after every word they write.
- Be sure that you use very generous spaces (especially with handouts) to give children enough room to write.

Teaching the Transition Group
l k y j

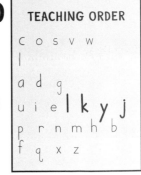

TEACHING ORDER

c o s v w
l
a d g
u i e l k y j
p r n m h b
f q x z

Key Points: Letters l k y j are similar to their capitals. Letters l and k start above the double lines, like t. Letters y and j go below the double lines. Use the lesson plan for l as a general guide for k y and j.

Letters and Numbers for Me
page 64

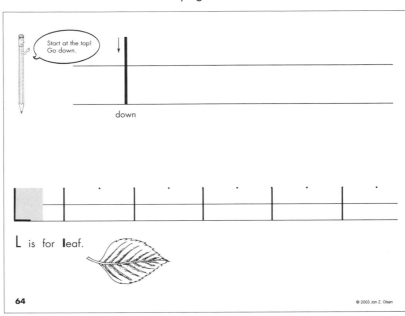

Start at the top! Go down.

down

L is for leaf.

64

© 2003 Jan Z. Olsen

Lesson Plan

Demonstrate l

Show children how to make l on the board and/or in the workbook.
Say the step-by-step directions as you demonstrate.

Teach in workbook

1. Find the picture of the pencil.
   Read the directions—"Start at the top. Go down."
   Finger trace the step-by-step model.
2. Find L on the gray block and l on the double lines.
   Copy the l's. Teacher should demonstrate, coach, and watch students.
   Note. Tell left-handed students to copy from the model on the right.
3. Read "L is for leaf." Move finger under the sentence from left to right.
   Find L and l in the sentence. Children may color the leaf and draw and lemon.

Tips

- Teach that l is a tall lowercase letter. Make a fist and say, "These are lowercase letters, but the lowercase l is tall." Then raise your index finger.
- Teach students to start exactly on the dot.

Evaluate

- If l is too short:
  Tell students to begin l high above the lines.

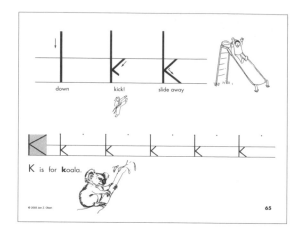

down   kick!   slide away

K is for **k**oala.

65

Teaching k

- K and k are similar.
- Teach that the kick in lowercase k is lower.
- This story helps children learn k. "The big line is Mr. Kaye, your karate teacher. He wants you to demonstrate a kick. Put the pencil on the line. That's you. Now kick Mr. Kaye. That's the karate k."

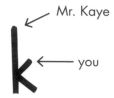

Mr. Kaye

you

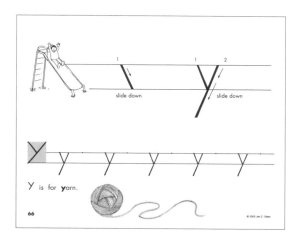

slide down   slide down

Y is for **y**arn.

66

Teaching y

- Lowercase y is like capital Y but is placed lower.
- Teach that y goes down below the line.
- If student slides the stroke the wrong way:
  Count very slowly: One . . . . . Two . . . . Which comes first? One! Make one slide down a short slide first. Slide the way the boy in the picture is sliding.

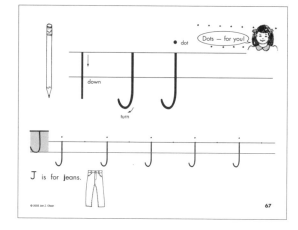

dot   Dots — for you!

down

turn

J is for **j**eans.

67

Teaching j

- J and j are similar, but point out the differences—they start in different places. They have different tops.
- If J or j curves too much:
  Make a "ruler" straight line down. Turn only at the bottom. Remind the child that j turns the same way as g.
- Teach that j goes down below the line.

Practicing Words and Sentences

Letters and Numbers for Me
pages 68 and 69

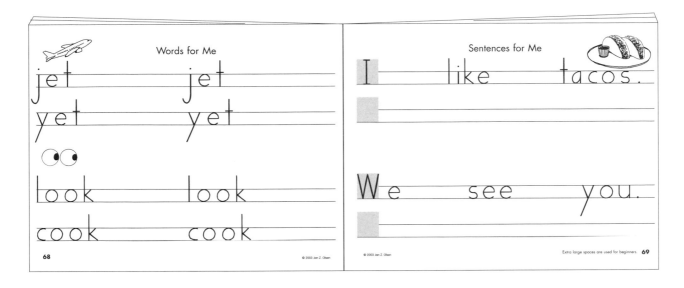

Words for Me

jet   jet

yet   yet

look   look

cook   cook

68

© 2003 Jan Z. Olsen

Sentences for Me

I like tacos.

We see you.

© 2003 Jan Z. Olsen

Extra large spaces are used for beginners. **69**

- Find the twin words.
- Read the words.
- Leave a generous space before beginning to copy words.
- Copy words from left to right.
- Students copy each word one time. (Help left-handed students to look at the middle list.)
- Students copy just two to four words a day. Copy from the first column one day and the second column the next.

- Begin sentences with a capital letter on the gray block.
- Students copy directly under each word.
- Leave space between words! The sentences use very generous spaces. Exaggerating the spaces now will result in beautiful sentence spacing as a habit.
- End with a period.

Teaching the Diver Letters
p r n m h b

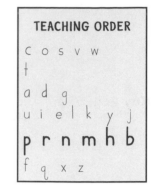

TEACHING ORDER

c o s v w
t
a d g
u i e l k y j
p r n m h b
f q x z

THE DIVER LETTERS

Let's pretend we're divers!
Stand up. Get ready!

Which way do you dive?
Down!

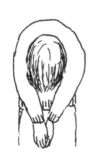

Then what happens?
You come up!

Then what do you do?
You swim over ...
on the top line!

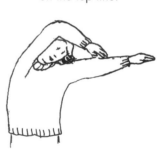

When you come up, be sure to swim over **on the top line**.

Demonstrate basic stroke patterns

The diver letters, p r n m h b, all begin with this sequence:
1. Dive down.
2. Come up.
3. Swim over to the right.

To teach this group, follow the illustration. Have your class stand up, go through the steps of diving down, coming up, and swimming over to the right side.

Demonstrate each letter with your finger

Face your class and draw a huge p in the air, saying "dive down, come up, swim over, and around." Have your students point to your index finger, following your motions. Repeat this demonstration with the other diver letters. Kids get a kick out of imaginary erasing between letters.

Important tip

When facing the class be sure to make the letters swim over to your left so they'll be right for your children. See above illustration.

Teaching the Diver Letters
p r n m h b

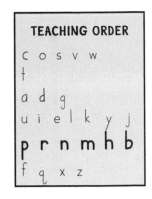
TEACHING ORDER

c o s v w
t
a d g
u i e l k y j
p r n m h b
f q x z

Key Points: Lowercase p r n m h b are Diver Letters. They begin with the same basic stroke pattern—dive down, come up, swim over. Use the lesson plan for p as a general guide for r n m h and b.

Letters and Numbers for Me
page 70

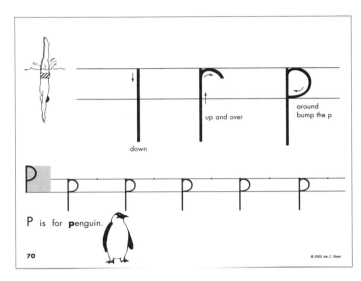

Lesson Plan

Demonstrate p

Show children how to make p on the board and/or in the workbook.
Say the step-by-step directions as you demonstrate.

Teach in workbook

1. Find the picture of the diver.
Read the directions—"Down, up, and over, around, bump the p."
Finger trace the step-by-step model.
2. Find P on the gray block and p on the double lines.
Copy the p's. Teacher should demonstrate, coach, and watch students.
Note: Tell left-handed students to copy from the model on the right.
3. Read "P is for penguin." Move finger under sentence from left to right.
Find P and p in the sentence.
P is for purple. Children may trace the p's with a purple crayon.

Tips

- Teach that P and p are in different positions.
- Teach that p goes down below the double lines.
- Capital P was taught with two strokes, but lowercase p is made with a continuous stroke.
- Have students stand and repeat diver motions, "Diver letters dive down, come up, and swim over." Write the letter p in the air for them to finger trace with you.

Evaluate

- If retracing is a problem:
Say they are in a diving competition. They must dive down and come straight up in the same bubbles.
- Remember to swim to the very top of the water (the top line).

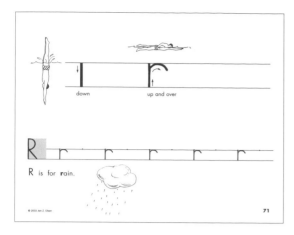

Teaching r

- Teach that R and r are different.
- Teach that r fits between the double lines.
- Letter r is made with a continuous stroke.
- Have students stand and repeat diver motions, "Diver letters dive down, come up, and swim over." Write the letter r in the air for them to finger trace with you.
- If r isn't retraced:
  Say the pencil must retrace until it gets to the top line and can swim over.

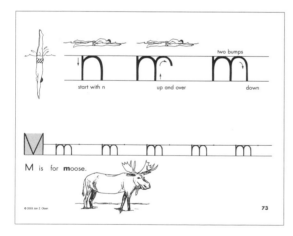

Teaching n

- Teach that N and n are different.
- Teach that n fits between the double lines.
- Letter n is made with a continuous stroke.
- Have students stand and repeat diver motions, "Diver letters dive down, come up, and swim over." Write the letter n in the air for them to finger trace with you.
- If n isn't retraced:
  The pencil must retrace until it gets to the top line and can swim over.

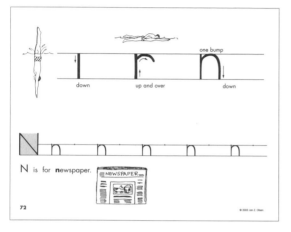

Teaching m

- Teach that M and m are different.
- Teach that m fits between the double lines.
- Letter m is made with a continuous stroke.
- If m has gaps, remind the children to dive down, come back up in the same bubbles, and swim over. If the bumps are too pointy, come up and "swim over" on the top line before going down again.
- If m has gaps, refer to a trash can! If people throw trash in those gaps it would become a stinky m. Tell the students, "These gaps collect trash. That's a stinky m."
  Close the gaps to keep the bumps together. Leave just enough room for a chocolate kiss.

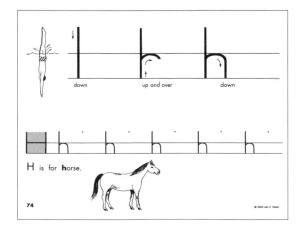

Teaching h

- Teach that H and h are different.
- Letter h is a high diver letter, it begins above the double lines.
- Letter h is made with a continuous stroke.
- If retracing is a problem:
  The pencil must retrace until it gets to the top line and can "swim over."
- If h finishes with a slide:
  Walk over on the top line, then straight down. No sliding allowed.

Teaching b

- Teach that B and b are different.
- Letter b is another high diver letter; it begins above the double lines.
- Letter b is made with a continuous stroke.
- Letter b begins like h.
- Write the letter h in the air for them to finger trace with you.
  Then do it again and say you have a surprise.
  Here is an h for a honey b. Make h turn into b.
  Never teach b and d together.

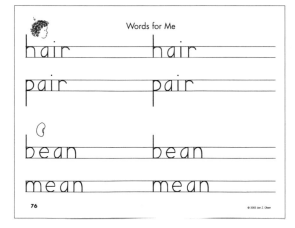

Words for Me
- Find the twin words.
- Read the words.
- Leave a generous space before beginning to copy words.
- Copy words from left to right.
- Students copy each word one time. (Help left-handed students to look at the middle list.)
- Students copy just two to four words a day. Copy from the first column one day and the second column the next.
- Practice sounding out the rhyming words.

Teaching the Final Group
f q x z

TEACHING ORDER

c o s v w
t
a d g
u i e l k y j
p r n m h b
f q x z

Key Points: This is the final group. Letter f is taught here because it has a difficult starting stroke. Letter q is taught here to avoid confusion with g. Capital partners x and z are saved for the end because of their infrequent use. Use this lesson plan for f as a general guide for q x and z.

Letters and Numbers for Me
page 77

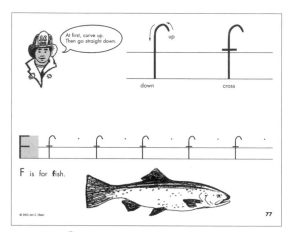

At first, curve up. Then go straight down.

up

down   cross

F is for fish.

© 2003 Jan Z. Olsen   77

Lesson Plan

Demonstrate f

Show children how to make f on the board and/or in the workbook.
Say the step-by-step directions as you demonstrate.

Teach in workbook

1. Find the picture of the fireman.
   The fireman says, "At first curve up. Then, straight down."
   Read the directions—"Up, down, cross."
   Finger trace the step-by-step model.
2. Find F on the gray block and f on the double lines.
   Copy the f's. Teacher should demonstrate, coach, and watch students.
   Note: Tell left-handed students to copy from the model on the right.
3. Read "F is for fish." Move finger under the sentence from left to right.
   Find F and f in the sentence. Children may color the fish.

Tips

- F and f are different.
- Teach the stroke for f by talking about water squirting out of a fire hose. It goes up and then falls down. Most water fountains also squirt up and fall down in an f curve. A first-hand experience at the water fountain can help children visualize the f.
- Teach students to start exactly on the dot and curve up.
- Children cross f according to their handedness:
  Right-handed children cross from left to right.
  Teacher marks ⟶ for right handed students.
  Left-handed children cross from right to left (pulling into the hand).
  Teacher marks ⟵ for left handed students.

Evaluate

- Does f start correctly?
  Help students begin by going up, then turning and falling straight down.

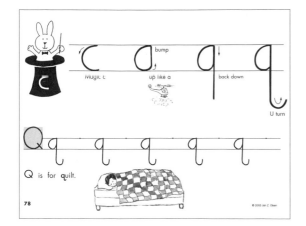

Teaching q

- Q and q are different.
- Teach that q goes below the double lines.
- In words, q is always followed by the letter u. Tell children to make a u-turn at the bottom of the q.
- Lowercase q is a "Magic c" letter but is introduced at the end to avoid confusion with g.
- Letter q is made with a continuous stroke.

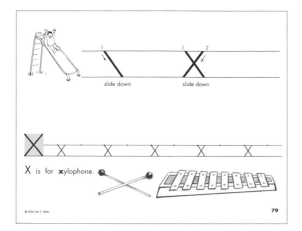

Teaching x

- Lowercase x is the same as X, just lower.
- Letter x fits between the double lines.
- If diagonal lines are a problem:
  Use the slate Wet–Dry–Try method.
- If x is made incorrectly:
  Use the slate or gray blocks. Letter x starts at the starting corner. The second line begins at the other top corner.

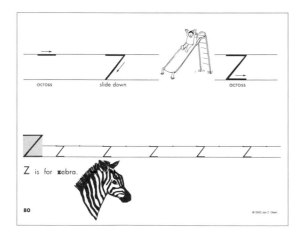

Teaching z

- Lowercase z is the same as Z, just lower.
- Letter z fits between the double lines.
- If z is reversed:
  Teach z on the slate. It starts in the starting corner.
  For right-handed children, they can pretend the left hand is chasing the z at the beginning.

Practicing Words and Sentences

Letters and Numbers for Me

Words for Me – page 76

- Find the twin words.
- Read the words.
- Leave a generous space before beginning to copy words.
- Copy words from left to right.
- Students copy each word one time. (Help left-handed students to look at the middle list.)
- Students copy just two to four words a day. Copy from the first column one day and the second column the next.

Sentences for Me – pages 82 and 83

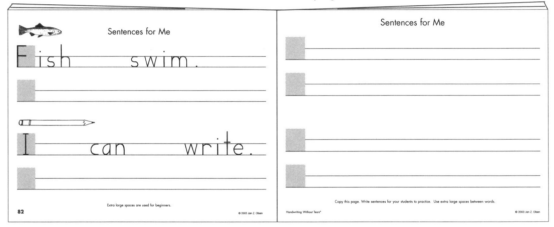

- Begin sentences with a capital letter on the gray block.
- Students copy directly under each word.
- Leave space between words! The sentences use very generous spaces. Exaggerating the spaces now will result in beautiful sentence spacing as a habit.
- End with a period.
- Photocopy the blank Sentences for Me page for extra practice.

My Name – page 84

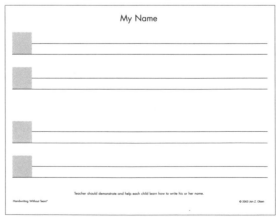

- Teacher should demonstrate and help each child learn to write his or her first name.
- Begin with a capital letter on the gray block and then use lowercase letters.
- Photocopy this page for practice as needed.

What now? Continue with very short daily lessons to maintain and improve printing skills. An easy way to plan your lessons is to focus on a different skill for each day of the week.

Monday: Capital Letters

Focus on capital letters. Capitals seldom get enough attention so do them first!

1. **Fill in the missing letters**
   The teacher may write any combination on the board.

   A _ C _ E _ G _ I _ K _ M _ O _ Q _ S _ U _ W _ Y _

2. **Write road, safety, and information signs**
   Use capital letters. Look for capitals at school!

   STOP   EXIT   FIRE   GIRLS   BOYS   BUS   HOT

3. **Play the Mystery Letter Game for Frog Jump Capitals**
   This slate activity on page 41 of this guide teaches children to start letters at the top. This activity also corrects reversals. Using a small piece of chalk on the slate develops the correct pencil grip.

4. **Review** F E D P B R N M
   Use page 9 from *Letters and Numbers for Me* to play the Mystery Letter Game on the gray blocks. This is a paper/pencil equivalent of the slate activity above.

5. **Review diagonal capitals—** A K M N V W **—with states**
   Using a wood puzzle of the USA, pass out state puzzle pieces. Children trace the puzzle piece on paper and write the appropriate capital letter on the state. Many states begin with diagonal letters A, K, M, N, V or W. Later, help your students write the correct two letter abbreviations. Modify this activity for other countries.

6. **An alphabetical roll call**
   Take roll to review capitals. Make copies of page 33 from *Letters and Numbers for Me*. Call out the letter A. If there is a student in the class whose name begins with A, the children write A below the A. If not, skip A. Continue through the alphabet. Then, color the selected gray blocks with a crayon. Fill in other letters later.

7. **A capital search**
   Review the rule about using a capital for the first letter of a sentence. Teach children how to find capitals at the beginning of sentences. The teacher copies a simple paragraph from a book. The children search for capitals at the beginning of sentences. They highlight or underline the capitals. Look for other capitals and teach the rules that apply.

8. **"Sign In Please"**
   Use the activity found on page 14 of this guide. You can change how children sign in to teach other skills. Develop circle skills by circling the letter by starting at the top with a C stroke.

Tuesday: Lowercase Letters

Focus on forming and placing lowercase letters correctly.

1. **Magic c Letters** — c o a d g
   Show children how you can make a Magic c Bunny out of a napkin. See page 67 of this guide for directions. Then, have the bunny help you play the Mystery Game for "Magic c" Letters (a, o, d, and g). Find it on page 57 of *Letters and Numbers for Me*.

2. **Diver Letters** — p r n m h b
   Stand up! Lead the children through the motions for the "diver letters" (p r n m h and b). These letters use the "down, up and over" stroke pattern. Write the six diver letters on paper (at back of guide).

Let's pretend we're divers! Stand up. Get ready!

Which way do you dive? **Down!**

Then what happens? **You come up!**

Then what do you do? **You swim over** ... on the top line!

3. **Same as Capitals** — c o s v w x z
   Use the multi-sensory Wet–Dry–Try method on the slate to teach these letters. Then have children write C c, O o, S s, V v, W w, X x, and Z z. This teaches the size difference between capital and lowercase letters.

4. **Missing Letters**
   Write letters on the board or paper and have children fill in the missing letters. This reviews the alphabet and helps children with placing letters.

   To review the small lowercase letters: _ b _ d _ f g h _ j k l _ _ _ p q _ _ t _ _ _ _ y z
   To review placing the tall letters: a _ c _ e _ g _ i j _ _ m n o p q r s _ u v w x y z
   To review placing descending letters: a b c d e f _ h i _ k l m n o _ _ r s t u v w x _ z

5. **Where Do You Start Your Letters? At the top!**
   This activity will guide children into correct habits for starting letters. Prepare: Make a page of double line paper (at back of guide) with 6 dots evenly spaced across the top lines. Get ready: Children put their pencils on the first dot and wait on the dot. Write: The teacher randomly calls out a letter - a c i m n o r s u v w x or z. Do one or two lines a day. This activity prevents children from starting letters on the bottom line.

6. **Review** e o t a n s
   These are the five most frequently used letters. See page 61 of this guide for more letters.

7. **Teach** T **and** t
   Letter t is tall like T. Have students make capital T with their arms as shown on page 65 of this guide. Then make lowercase t by crossing the t lower. Say that T and t are tall but lowercase t is crossed lower.

Wednesday: Words

W is for words and Wednesday!
Focus on putting letters in the word close together and leaving spaces between words.

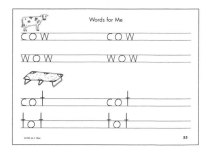

1. **Printing Letters In a Word**
   Letters in a word are close to each other. Focus on this by having the children put their index fingers close together, but not touching. Remind children that letters within words need to be this close!

2. **Sick Word Clinic**
   Write a sick word on the board – c   a   t – and have the children fix it by copying it over with the letters close to each other.

3. **Words with the Magic c letters –** o   a   d   g
   If you reviewed a, d, g, or o on Tuesday, then try some of these words on Wednesday: cow, cat, call, add, act, age, dad, dog, dig, go, gas, gag, old, oar, oat

4. **Words with the diver letters –** p   r   n   m   h   b
   If you reviewed p, r, n, m, h, b on Tuesday, then try some rhyming words with diver letters: man, pan; rub, hub; rib, bib; arm, farm; run, bun; hen, pen.

5. **Write the word that goes with each picture.**

   cow
   whale
   fish
   dog

   _____   _____   _____   _____

6. **Birthday Names**
   Make a simple birthday card. Show children how to print the birthday child's name by demonstrating it on the board. You may even teach an exclamation mark to be used after the name. Children can sign the cards and give them to the birthday child.

   Happy Birthday _____

   From _____

7. **Frequently Used Words**
   Practice writing important, frequency used words from the Dolch list. Find these words by searching for Dolch lists on the web.

8. **Words with letter q.**
   The seldom-used letter q is also a Magic c letter. Teach children to make a "u" turn at the bottom of the q and follow q with u. Write quick, quiet, quack, or quote.

87

Thursday: Sentences

Thoughts on Thursday! A sentence is a complete thought. Teach sentence skills today.

1. Watch the Teacher and Write

Beginning sentence skills are most easily achieved if you demonstrate letter-by-letter, word-by-word, and space-by-space. Write one sentence for your class or student to imitate. Use the "Sentences for Me" page at the back of *Letters and Numbers for Me* or Wide Double Line Paper.

2. Sentence Spacing with Pennies

Give your children pennies or chips to use. Teach them how to look at a short simple sentence and fix the pennies to match as in this example.

I   SEE   A   DOG.

3. Sick Sentence Clinic

The teacher writes a sentence with the letters too far apart. Circle each word in the sentence. Now copy the sentence over, putting the letters closer. For example:

I a m b i g. $\longrightarrow$ I am big.

Now, write a sentence with the letters too close. Children underline each word in the sentence. Leave space between words. Now copy the sentence over with spaces between the words.

Icanrun. $\longrightarrow$ I can run.

Friday: Fun with Numbers

Review numbers with fantastic activities today.

1. Re-teach a number with the multi-sensory Wet–Dry–Try method found on page 34 in the workbook, *Letters and Numbers for Me.*

2. Supervise as children write numbers 1 through 10 using page 45 from *Letters and Numbers for Me.*

3. Put a smiley face in the top left corner of the door frame. Tell children that the smiley face is the starting corner for 1 2 3 4 5 6 and 7. Point to the smiley face and then write numbers "on the door," but actually in the air.

4. Write phone numbers or street addresses of your school.

5. Teach children to write today's date or write numbers on a calendar.

6. Count and write numbers. Have small objects to count and record.

Note to Teachers and Parents

Everyone at Handwriting Without Tears® wishes you much success as you work with your children. Please vist our website for more teaching tips and our current workshop schedule. We are always happy to hear from you and welcome your comments and suggestions. Thank you!

Jan Z. Olsen

Jan Z. Olsen, OTR • Handwriting Without Tears® • 8001 MacArthur Blvd • Cabin John, MD 20818
JanOlsen@hwtears.com • www.hwtears.com

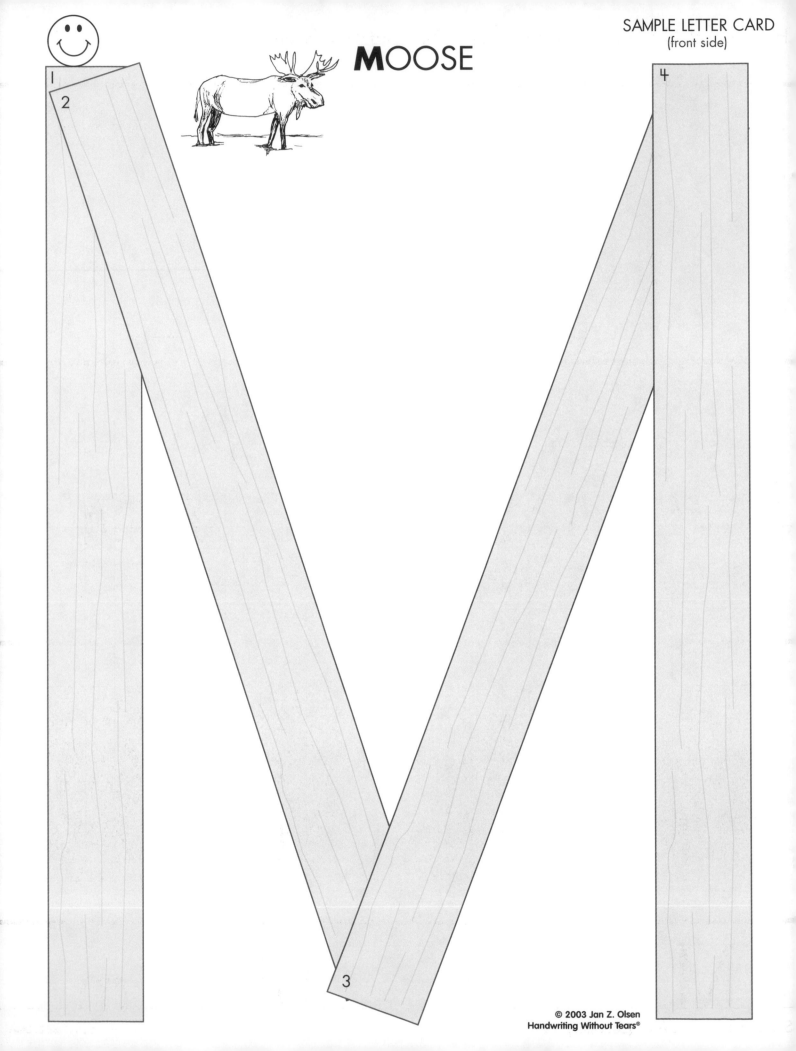

MOOSE

Help your children to look at the first one. Then find the one that is the same.

HWT GRAY BLOCKS
FOR CAPITALS AND NUMBERS